THE DOUBLE IMAGE
CONCEPTS OF THE POET
IN SLAVIC LITERATURES

THE DOUBLE IMAGE

CONCEPTS OF THE POET IN SLAVIC LITERATURES

By VICTOR ERLICH

THE JOHNS HOPKINS PRESS
BALTIMORE, MARYLAND

This book has been brought to publication with the assistance of a grant from The Ford Foundation.

TO IZA

ACKNOWLEDGMENTS

While working on this book, I have had an opportunity to discuss its central theme with a number of friends and colleagues, Slavists and non-Slavists alike. In fact, since in several essays I have ventured beyond the area of my special competence, the substantive and bibliographical suggestions offered by students of English romanticism, classicists and psychiatrists have been very essential to me. I am particularly grateful to Fritz Schmidl for his thoughtful comments and for his calling my attention to the important book about the myth of the artist by Kris and Kurz. Needless to say, none of these scholars should be held responsible for the opinions expressed or the interpretations urged here. But I am indebted to all of them for their interest in my work and the illumination which they have often provided.

During the last three or four years my preoccupation with the subject of this book inevitably spilled into some of the courses or seminars which I taught at the University of Washington and at Yale. The response of my students has been gratifying; it has provided an additional spur to finishing the oft-interrupted job.

It was my good fortune to have received steady and intelligent support at home as well. My mother, Sophie Dubnov-Erlich, has shared with me some of her first-hand knowledge of the poetic revival and the general ambiance of the Russian "Silver age." My wife to whom these essays are gratefully dedicated has offered incisive criticism and encouragement which never flagged throughout the periods of gestation and of actual writing.

The early phase of the research embodied in this volume was made possible by a Guggenheim award for the summer and fall of 1958. The more recent stages of the process were supported by grants from the Far Eastern and Russian Institute of the University of Washington. I am grateful to the Guggenheim Foundation for its support and confidence, and to my former University of Washington colleagues, especially George E. Taylor and Donald W. Treadgold, for their generous assistance and, perhaps, more important, for that atmosphere of intellectual vitality, of commitment to ideas, which over the long years of my association with the Institute I had come to value so highly.

Some of the material contained here has been previewed in learned journals. The bulk of the concluding essay "Life by Verses: Boris Pasternak" appeared as "The Concept of the Poet in Pasternak," in the June, 1959 issue of *The Slavonic and East European Review.* "The Dead Hand of the Future" was featured in the September, 1962 issue of *The Slavic Review.* Finally a large portion of "The Cost of the Image" was published in *Studies in Romanticism* (Vol. I, Summer, 1962, No. 4) under the title "The Concept of the Poet in Krasiński and the Romantic Myth of the Artist."

In transliterating from the Russian throughout this book the Library of Congress system has been used.

V. E.

Seattle, Washington
August 1963.

CONTENTS

THE DOUBLE IMAGE
CONCEPTS OF THE POET
IN SLAVIC LITERATURES

1. THE DOUBLE IMAGE

" Der Künstler . . . doch ein Wesen besonderer
Art ist — erhaben, selbstherrlich, verrucht,
zeitweilig recht unbegreiflich " (Freud).[1]

The essays which follow are brief reconsiderations of six Slavic poets. The first two—Aleksandr Pushkin and the Polish poet and playwright Zygmunt Krasiński—belong to the Romantic era. The remaining four—Valerii Briusov, Aleksandr Blok, Vladimir Maiakovskii and Boris Pasternak—are leading representatives of Russian Symbolist and post-Symbolist poetry, respectively.

In dealing with these disparate and in part chronologically discontinuous poetic careers no attempt will be made to tell a consecutive story, to weave a coherent pattern. Yet if the present volume has no thesis, it does have a focus. The essays which it comprises are held together by the unity of the vantage point, by a common theme—that of the image, or self-image, of the poet.

To avoid misunderstandings and false expectations, let me make clear that the term " self-image " as used here is not primarily a psychological or biographical notion. What is at issue is not the individual poet's view of himself as a human being but a more abstract and ideational entity—notably the concept of the poet as an ideal type which informs the given artist's work and helps shape his life.

[1] Sigmund Freud, *Briefe, 1893–1939* (Frankfurt am Main, 1960).

1

To be sure, the artist's doctrinal commitment bears a definable, if not always direct, relation to his psychic makeup. As I will attempt to show in my discussion of two Russian Symbolists,[2] this connection often is a two-way street. If the poet's personality is likely to affect his choice of an operative model or myth, this choice in turn is bound to influence his actual behavior, at least to the extent of providing a post-factum rationale for a congenital temperamental proclivity. While some attention will be paid to this dialectical interplay,[3] the image or self-image of the poet will be interpreted here primarily as an element of a literary ideology, as a facet of an over-all aesthetic and intellectual orientation, of a poetics.

It is by now a commonplace that each school of poetry has its own conception of the nature and uses of poetic creation. Ever since the Renaissance each of the successive or contending literary movements, or for that matter, individual masters, has made its own characteristic selection from the culturally available solutions to the perennial dilemma of the poet caught forever between prophecy and craft, commitment and detachment, public responsibility and private delight, self-expression and mimesis, high seriousness and play. "Poetry in its original culture-making capacity," says the brilliant Dutch historian Johan Huizinga in *Homo Ludens*,[4] "is born in and as play— sacred play, no doubt, but always, even in its sanctity verging on gay abandon, mirth and jollity."

"Sacred play," a telling and remarkably apposite oxymoron. Indeed it can be argued that the tension between the adjective and the noun in Huizinga's formula is at the core of many

---

[2] See below, "The Maker and the Seer," pp. 68–119.

[3] The same dialectical relationship seems to obtain between the poet's image of himself and the concepts of the artist current in his milieu. In making his existential choice the poet is inevitably affected by the values of his literary or larger environment, of his "ism," his time and his class. But if he is Goethe, Byron, Hugo, or Pushkin, that is a commanding, event-making figure, he does not merely exemplify prevalent assumptions about the poet, but helps shape them as well.

[4] *Homo Ludens* (Boston, 1950), p. 122.

dichotomies which traditionally have clustered around the poetic act.

I shall revert in the following essay to the apparent contrast highlighted by Huizinga—that between the ultimately serious import of poetry and the poet's inevitably playful attitude toward his medium. Let me say at this point that the very structure of the above phrase makes it a singularly appropriate point of departure for a discussion of the images of the poet and of poetry current in Western culture. At once "useless" and yet somehow indispensable, alternately marginal and central, thriving on illusion, artifice, make-believe and yet intimately and powerfully involved with various human faculties and interests, autonomous and self-contained and yet uniquely capable of emulating and illuminating the texture of reality, frivolous and self-indulgent and yet remarkably adept at dramatizing society's most essential values, art, or more specifically poetry, has been perhaps the most baffling and contradiction ridden of all major human activities.

The paradoxical nature of poetry has found its counterpart in the precarious status of the poet. Alternately worshiped as a seer and patronized as a "mere" entertainer, or worse still, denounced as an irresponsible troublemaker, he has been forever a disconcerting figure to Keats's "Men of Power" who have had considerable trouble deciding whether they should ignore him, try to get rid of him or to use him. Had the poet been merely whimsical, he could have been easily dismissed as an idle flute player. It is the strange mixture of "irrelevance" with technical virtuosity and a spellbinding power that make him a cause for concern, a target of perplexed ambivalence. An unguided missile of unknown destination and unfathomable impact, he has seemed to confront the organization man with an insidious threat and a subtle temptation.

Probably the most influential statement of the centuries-old ambivalence toward the poet was provided by Plato. In a much-commented-on passage in *Ion* the poet's divine madness or "enthusiasm" (interpreted by ancient Greeks as possession, frenzy) appears to be a mixed blessing. Both poets and rhapsodists utter what they do by a divine dispensation. ". . . For the poet is a light and winged and holy thing, and there is no invention in him until he has been inspired and *out of his senses* [my italics] and the mind is no longer in him; when he has not attained this status, he is powerless to utter his oracles."[5] When inspired from on high, the poet soars above the common herd; yet when left to his own devices, he is "powerless," he knows less than the normal man. To put it differently, the poet is at once superior to the ordinary mortal in that he is in touch with the higher powers, and inferior because of the paucity of his own resources and a lower degree of control over, and awareness of, his own feelings. Capacity for intermittent self-transcendence and prophecy clearly exacts a heavy price.

In the famous attack on the poet featured in Plato's *The Republic*, intellectual inadequacy, on balance, appears to be a less serious charge than is that of emotional unreliability, indeed subversiveness. Poetry, warns Plato, especially dramatic poetry, has the most formidable power of corrupting even men of high character. By his uncritical fixation on the imperfect sensory data not purified by the controlling reason, the poet encourages a surrender of the intellect to the chaotic flux of phenomena. Moreover—and perhaps more important—by his uncannily effective, indeed contagious imitation (mimesis) of violent emotions, he undermines the discipline and self-possession incumbent upon the rational man.

In his recent book[6] Eric A. Havelock argues quite persuasively that some of Plato's accusations cannot be properly understood or evaluated without reference to the cultural situation to which he is addressing himself. Havelock properly reminds us that in pre-Platonic Greece, especially throughout its oral stage, poetry was the chief source of moral guidance and

[5] *Ion* 534b, 3 (Burnet).
[6] *Preface to Plato* (London, 1963).

of knowledge about the world, the "sole vehicle of important and significant communication."[7] Seen in this perspective, many of Plato's strictures may well be interpreted as polemics with traditional claims in behalf of poetry's cognitive and educational value, claims which many of us would be inclined to dub extravagant or unwarranted.

Havelock's argument strikes me as a salutary antidote to some blatantly ahistorical interpretations of Plato's ethos such as the recent attempt to present the Greek philosopher as a precursor of fascism.[8] Yet when all due allowances are made for the essential differences in the actual status of the poet between Homeric Greece and, say, nineteenth-century England, some of Plato's injunctions and warnings retain a remarkably— if perhaps deceptively—modern ring. Suffice it to mention the conflict implicit in the argument of *The Republic* between the unambiguous starkness of philosophical truth or scientific knowledge and the seductive glitter of the poetic illusion, between the poet's delight in variety, ambiguity and contradiction and the systematic thinker's rage for order, unity and coherence. There is, too, in Plato the stern moralist's distrust of the emotional unpredictability of the impulse-oriented "lovers of sounds and sights" and, last but not least, the much-cited readiness to ban the poets from the republic unless they learn to curb their subversive proclivities and put their free-wheeling magic to constructive use. "You must be quite sure we can admit into our commonwealth only the poetry which celebrates the praises of the gods and of good men."[9] The only kind of poetry which is tolerable to the community is one that promotes communal objectives. Imaginative literature can be absorbed into the body politic only if it can be made to serve as a mode of edification, only when it is emasculated, or better still, harnessed.

---

[7] *Ibid.*, p. 93.

[8] See the authors referred to in Ronald B. Levinson, *In Defense of Plato*, Ch. IX (Cambridge, Mass., 1953).

[9] *The Republic of Plato* (London, 1945), p. 339.

Does this not sound painfully familiar? Without minimizing the difference between the grandeur of Plato's vision and the tedious vulgarity of a totalitarian politician one cannot help but note a remarkable continuity of underlying assumptions as between the above dicta and an assertion made by Nikita Khrushchev in the course of his recent attack on the Soviet intellectuals: "Our people cannot use this rubbish [dedaca-cophonous music] as a tool of their ideology."[10]

The apprehensiveness about the role and the nature of the poet so forcefully articulated by Plato is part of a larger phenomenon—the double image of the artist. In their valuable study *Die Legende vom Künstler*[11] Ernst Kris and Otto Kurz probe thoughtfully the "enigma of the Artist as a sociopsychological phenomenon." The authors marshal telling evidence, drawn in large part from ancient Greek legends about sculptors and painters, to document the inherent duality of the "myth of the artist" endemic in Western culture, shuttling as it does between awe and distrust, adulation and denigration.

As Kris and Kurz correctly point out, at the twilight of classical antiquity the former attitude received a strong impetus from neo-Platonism. If Plato's rationalism was wary of the lures of poetic magic, Plotinus' brand of idealism which set more store by inward vision than by outward reality, by imagination than by mimesis, clearly pointed toward an apotheosis of artistic creativity. Within the neoidealistic scheme the work of art appears not as a pale approximation of reality, but as its transformation, which by doing away with the contingent defects of nature, comes closer than nature ever could to the ideal of aesthetic perfection.[12] Thus emerges what Kris and Kurz call *die Geniereligion*, a religion which deifies the artist. The Renaissance, which worshiped creative energy,

---

[10] Quoted from "Khrushchev on Culture," *Encounter*, pamphlet 9 (1963), p. 30.

[11] *Die Legende vom Künstler* (Wien, 1934).

[12] Cf., E. Panofsky, *Ein Beitrag zur Begriffsgeschichte der älteren Kunsttheorie* (Leipzig, 1924).

codified the cult of the genius into a notion of the artist as a demiurge. " This prerogative," says Kris in a more recent book,[13] " determines the manner in which the Artist is heroized. Renaissance artists asserted their sovereignty in depicting themselves as ' God and Creator ' (*dio et creatore*) of the work of art (Leonardo) ; and their environment, in turn, unhesitatingly bestowed upon them the attitude ' divine ' (*divino*)." The bold analogy worked both ways: if the artist was likened to the Creator, the latter was often referred to as a cosmic artist. " To Leónardo da Vinci the world is a masterpiece, God the supreme builder." [14]

Yet within the Judaeo-Christian tradition, claiming for a fellow human or for oneself a Godlike omnipotence admittedly is a perilous matter—an act of blasphemy or of Satanic pride. Thus, for centuries the *divino artista* image has been accompanied by its reverse—that of a usurper or interloper, typically a sorcerer deriving his uncanny powers from a secret alliance with dark forces. For obvious reasons this ominous notion loomed large in the Middle Ages when a pre-Christian poet such as Virgil was typically seen not only as a heathen, but also a bad magician, an ally or tool of the Evil One. The theocratic ethos of medieval Europe cast the secular artist in the role of a Faustian figure: his thirst for omnipotence or omniscience was a sacrilege, his unhallowed virtuosity was suspect; it smacked of black magic.

As Kris and Kurz clearly demonstrate, this negative archetype, as so many others, can be traced back to ancient Greece. Greek mythology abounds in tales about challengers or " apes " of the Gods. Daedalus, Prometheus and Hephaestus attempt now literally, now figuratively, to steal the Gods' thunder, peer into the forbidden realm. In one fashion or another all these over-reachers are struck down by the angry Gods, jealous of

---

[13] *Psychoanalytic Explorations in Art*, " The Image of the Artist " (New York, 1952), p. 79.
[14] Kris and Kurz, *Die Legende vom Künstler*, p. 58.

their prerogatives. The least known among them, Epimetheus is symbolically and appropriately degraded by being turned into an ape.[15]

Some of the Greek parables cited in *Die Legende vom Künstler* center around what is perhaps the most uncanny and forever unsettling element of the artist's magic—notably his unique ability to produce a complete illusion of reality, to trick the dazzled audience into mistaking the artifact for the real thing. The grapes on Zeuxis' painting or the curtain on Parrhasius' are so vivid and lifelike as to take in now a bride, now the painter's fellow craftsman. Likewise Heracles mistakes Daedalus' statue of himself for his own reflection.

In some mythical plots the motif of an optical illusion is supplanted by that of an actual transformation. The cliché about the lifelike quality of the products of the artist's imagination is taken literally in the Pygmalion-type myth about statues which come to life. "The capacity to create mobile and intelligent beings belongs, at least within the Greek cultural realm, to the prerogatives of the legendary artist." [16]

Need one add that some of these myths have found their way into modern fiction? The image of the artist as magician or of the magician as artist reappears in the malevolent spell cast upon his helpless audience by Thomas Mann's Mario and the Magician and in I. B. Singer's remarkably suggestive tale about the magician of Lublin poised precariously, in a spectacular tight-rope act, between heaven and hell. By the same token, the notion that the work of art is capable of assuming a life of its own, indeed of stealing the thunder from the real thing, is

---

[15] In her essay "The Image of the Artist" (*The Journal of Aesthetics and Art Criticism*, XXI, No. 2 [Winter, 1961]), Geraldine Peldes speaks of the "semi-legendary artist deeply embedded in mythological matrix, as a type of priest, sorcerer or physician who acquired a criminal cast from the forbidden nature of his activity which, as in Daedalus or Prometheus, conflicted with the power of the Demiurge, and from his identity as the possessor of magical power by means of a pact with Satan" (p. 25).

[16] Kris and Kurz, *Die Legende vom Künstler*, p. 74.

epitomized by the plot of Oscar Wilde's *The Portrait of Dorian Grey.*

One of the salient facts which emerges from explorations such as the one undertaken by Kris and Kurz is precisely the longevity of certain fundamental assumptions about or attitudes toward the creative genius. Through all the shifts in the sociocultural status of the artist, however significant and dramatic, there persisted the "double image of the artist as a wicked sorcerer and a mighty creator, an image at once admirable and threatening" (*bewundert* and *gefährlich*).[17]

More broadly, there are few notions about the artist or the poet, current during the last two centuries, that could not be traced back to the Renaissance if indeed not to ancient Greece. The images of the poet as priest, soothsayer or spiritual leader, as demiurge, as corruptor of youth, and finally as "mere" artificer were bequeathed to the modern era by the earlier ages.

Yet the distinctive contribution of the nineteenth century, especially of its Romantic phase, should not be underestimated. Romanticism which proclaimed the "belief that the artist is . . . a full realization of the human potential"[18] powerfully activated some of the time-honored concepts by placing them at the center of the literary sensibility of the age. The view of poetry as prophecy and of the poet as a bard was given a new lease on life in Victor Hugo's charismatic posturing, in Shelley's grandiloquent rhetoric, in the impact and predicament of the Polish Romantic poet, doomed to the "mastery of the souls" over an embattled people.[19] By the same token the negative facet of the archetype was revived with vengeance by that dark, Gothic strain in the Romantic tradition which has been so eagerly explored by Mario Praz and Leslie Fiedler.[20] Yet this

[17] *Ibid.*, p. 92.
[18] M. Z. Shroder, *Icarus, The Image of the Artist in French Romanticism* (Cambridge, Mass, 1961), p. 1.
[19] See below, "The Cost of the Image: The Strange Case of Zygmunt Krasiński," pp. 54–55.
[20] Mario Praz, *The Romantic Agony* (London, New York, 1951, 1954); Leslie Fiedler, *Love and Death in the American Novel* (New York, 1960).

time the ominous note was sounded in a new key. In Romantic satanism the demonic image of the poet is not an objectification of the layman's dread of poetry's unhallowed power, but the poet's own self-definition, a defiant challenge to the ordinary morality, flung with a mixture of perverse pride and anguish.

This shift of the vantage point is part of what has been called "the Romantic revolution." Though the poets' attempts at self-justification or, if one will, self-glorification, go as far back as Hesiod, the over-all difference of emphasis is only too apparent. What with the Romantic's heightened sense of the self, the image of the poet becomes increasingly the matter of the poet's self-image. It is thus that in much of the Romantic literature the environment's traditional ambivalence is internalized, that is, turned into an inner conflict, a shuttling between aesthetic narcissism, a Byronic pride in being different from the common herd, and a sense of moral uneasiness if not outright guilt over the poet's ineradicable frivolity, self-centeredness, and moral alienation.

The Romantic urge to recoil upon one's self was often bound up with the growing estrangement from societal values and a concomitant tendency—which will loom large in the pages that follow—to turn poetry into a central value, a shortcut to salvation. To quote M. Z. Shroder again, in the Romantic age "art itself came to mean more than the technique of poetry or of painting; it was a way of life, a quasi-religious concept." [21] "Delacroix," writes Geraldine Peldes in a wide-ranging essay, "sometimes spoke of the artist as a person who behaves in a certain way rather than as someone who practices a specific profession." [22] The poet's life—actual or mythologized—acquires a crucial importance.

The tendency to mean by "poetry" a mode of experience rather than a distinctive professional activity or body of creative accomplishment was to survive the Romantic move-

---

[21] Shroder, *Icarus*, p. 7.
[22] Peldes, "The Image of the Artist," p. 122.

ment. True, modern poetry has produced vigorous alternatives to the Romantic self-dramatization. The early T. S. Eliot's ideal of impersonality, the notion of poetry as "not a turning loose of emotion but an escape from emotions" is a significant manifestation of the twentieth-century reaction to the lyrical exhibitionism of some Romantics. Yet the career of another master of the English poetic idiom highlights what might be called a morbidly modern variant of the Romantic syndrome. Dylan Thomas' poetry, though intense and often personal, does not purport to project an image of a personal plight in the sense in which it is true of Paul Verlaine, Aleksandr Blok or Vladimir Maiakovskii. Yet it was precisely the predicament of the *poète maudit* as enacted in real life in the form of self-destructive antics and desperate clowning that has caught the imagination of Thomas' public, often at the expense of his poetry. The man seems to have stolen the show from the poet by assuming the role of a "scapehero" (Leslie Fiedler) who in his emotional disarray, in the chaotic, disheveled quality of personal life fulfills the secret wishes of many a solid citizen, acts out "rejected values of heedlessness, disorder and madness." [23]

When Thomas burned himself out, the myth swallowed up a major lyrical talent. No such claim could be made for any of the latter-day Bohemians, known as the Beat poets. The striking thing about the Beat movement is not that, except possibly for one or two of its poetic spokesmen, it has failed to produce any memorable verse. It is rather the fact that in this milieu it is possible to be considered a poet without having written a single poem. Once again "poetry" is interpreted as an existential commitment, an attitude rather than an activity, as living—or refusing to live—a certain kind of life.

As indicated above, only two of the poets under discussion belong chronologically to the Romantic age. (I am saying "chronologically" since it is still a matter of controversy among

[23] Fiedler, *Love and Death* . . . , p. 411.

Russian literary historians whether the greatest Russian poet could be properly labeled a Romantic.) The characteristically Romantic notion of poetry, and of the poet, will be most strikingly exemplified here by such post-Romantic figures as the Symbolist Aleksandr Blok and the Futurist Vladimir Maiakovskii. What Pasternak was to call in *Safe Conduct* the "Romantic image of the poet" [24] was a vital presence in all the modern Russian poets examined here, now as a model to be emulated or modified—sometimes, as in Maiakovskii, to the accompaniment of vociferous protestations—now as something to be eschewed or transcended, in either case an operative norm, a force to be reckoned with.

This remarkable tenacity of some Romantic assumptions and myths is only one of the larger implications of my inquiry into six Slavic poets. During the last two centuries Russian poetry has been part and parcel of European literature. The theme which links the essays has international relevance. No wonder the import of the poetic destinies pondered here points far beyond the Slavic literary scene. In fact, I would be inclined to argue that they epitomize some salient facets of the modern poet's situation with special clarity and poignancy.

Few masters of nineteenth-century literature can match Pushkin's free-wheeling ideational eclecticism, capable of encompassing nearly all the concepts of the poet available to the European literary mind at the beginning of the last century. Few Romantic or post-Romantic men of letters have projected their anguish over the artist's alleged emotional aridity with the explicitness of Zygmunt Krasiński's *The Undivine Comedy*. By the same token, few contemporary lyrists embraced the notion of the poet's life as a dramatic prefiguration of a future worthy of the artist with the desperate intensity of Aleksandr Blok or the Utopian fervor of Vladimir Maiakovskii.

[24] See below, "Life by Verses," pp. 133–34.

With Blok and Maiakovskii, especially with the latter, we confront a modern dilemma about which contemporary Russian literature has a great deal to tell us—notably, the dilemma of literature vs. politics or more specifically, the complex, often intimate yet hardly ever harmonious, relationship between the literary rebellion and revolutionary action.

The Romantic's repudiation of the given had assumed various forms ranging from the aristocratic traditionalism of Chateaubriand to Victor Hugo's flamboyant cult of progress, from Shelley's radical protest to Alfred de Vigny's pessimistic withdrawal. At times the individualistic rebellion of the Romantic artist and the tide of social reform seem to converge. To Victor Hugo romanticism was "liberalism in literature," that is, the natural ally, or the closest literary counterpart, of the movement of social emancipation. "Many artists," says Geraldine Peldes, " whether or not they participated directly in the social and political eruptions, regarded art itself as an avenue of revolutions, political and social." [25] As the century drew to its close, Hugo's libertarian euphoria gave way increasingly to de Vigny's weary aloofness from the social strife and to Flaubert's bitter scorn for " both your houses."

More recently, the violent rejection of the status quo by Bohemian artists unhinged and traumatized by World War I and its aftermath, overlapped, but never coalesced with a new wave of political radicalism. Among the symptoms of this hybrid ferment was the short-lived alliance of surrealism with Marxism in French poetry of the twenties, and the blatantly harsh, but contradiction-ridden communism of Bertolt Brecht, shot through by mutually cancelling ironies.

The brief encounter of the literary *avant-garde* with the political Left was spurred by the apocalyptic hopes engendered by the Russian Revolution. Clearly it is the twentieth-century Russian poetry that was most directly and crucially affected by

[25] Peldes, " The Image of the Artist," p. 131.

this momentous process. The atmosphere of crisis and disarray which prevailed in pre-1917 Russia, the reluctant disintegration of the oppressive and ineffectual tsarist regime, coupled with the Bohemian artist's hatred of "Philistinism" and the Russian intelligent's proclivity for total solutions, produced in many a Russian poet a fascination with doom, a mood of waiting for a purifying cataclysm, a hankering for the millennium. To a Russian Symbolist like Aleksandr Blok or Andrei Belyi the Revolution was a vehicle of frenzied eschatology. To Maiakovskii, a *déclassé* Dadaist turned Bolshevik, it epitomized a new beginning, a clean break with the "stifling past" which denied the rebellious artist air, fulfillment, a place under the sun. At different stages of that tumultuous engagement and in varying ways and degrees both Blok and Maiakovskii were to pay the price of disenchantment, of spiritual or actual suicide, for having ridden an alien, indeed hostile "wave of the future," for having entrusted the impossible task of liberating poetry from the tyranny of routine to grim-faced and profoundly antipoetic organization men.

By April, 1930, when Maiakovskii shot himself through the heart, the revolutionary chaos which he celebrated so resonantly had solidified into the mold of the most elaborate system of cultural repression in modern history. As distinguished from Babel, Tsvetaeva, Mandelshtam, and many other masters of modern Russian literature Maiakovskii was not primarily a victim of Stalinist dictatorship. But the date as well as some of the circumstances of his tragic death point up another facet of the modern poet's predicament which the Soviet man of letters had come to know more intimately than did most of his western European counterparts—notably, the fate of the poet under totalitarianism.

The poet's quarrel with the system under which he lives, with his society and his age is a time-honored theme. Because of the inherently problematical status of the poet and a thoroughly unpoetic frame of mind on the part of the bulk of the community, there have been few periods in the history of Western society which could not have been or, in fact, have not been construed, with some justification, as profoundly anti-poetic. (In "Masquerade," by Jarosław Iwaszkiewicz—a Polish play written between the two wars—one of the characters exclaims as he ponders the tragic news about Pushkin's death: "This is a country in which a poet cannot live!" A fellow mourner extends the scope of this indictment: "And is there a country where a poet *can* live?").

The exacerbated sense of the self and the growing distrust of the outside world characteristic of the nineteenth century literary mind reinvigorated this tension. Though it was hailed intermittently as an age of hope and progress, the nineteenth century received more than its fair share of abuse. A nostalgic Polish Romantic, Zygmunt Krasiński, spoke for many of his contemporaries when he denounced it as a "century of oppressors and bankers."[26] The twentieth century, the age of "extreme situations," has lent the poet's traditional grievances a special edge, a tragic poignancy. For it is in our day, most conspicuously and massively in Stalin's Russia, that the poet was confronted with a terrible choice between silence, if not actual annihilation, and spiritual betrayal. Osip Mandelshtam, who perished in a Soviet forced labor camp, a victim of the tyrant's personal vindictiveness, found a chillingly appropriate label for his era: "My age, the wolf-strangling beast, leaps upon my shoulders."[27]

Need I insist, in conclusion, on the symbolic significance of the last protagonist of our staggered tale, Boris Pasternak? If his achievement argues eloquently for the magnificent resilience of poetry, his ordeal is a grim reminder that ours are times which often try the poets' souls beyond the limit of human endurance.

---

[26] *Correspondence de S. Krasiński et Henry Reeve* (Paris, 1908), I, 188.
[27] *Sobranie sochinenii* (New York, 1955), p. 147.

2. SACRED PLAY
ALEKSANDR PUSHKIN

> "*The aim of poetry is poetry.*"
> (Pushkin, in a letter to a friend
> who was wondering about the "aim"
> of Pushkin's poem "The Gypsies.")

1.

To speak about the concept of the poet in Pushkin is to enter the realm to which Huizinga's pithy definition of poetry's "culture-making" function is singularly applicable: ". . . Sacred play, . . . always, even in its sanctity, verging on gay abandon, mirth and jollity."[1]

Perhaps, before I go any further I should try to clarify my terms of reference. To quote Huizinga once more, "the contrast between play and seriousness is always fluid."[2] The play-concept need not suggest frivolity or mere entertainment. What it does invariably entail is toying with, and a disinterested delight in, the man-made forms and textures of a make-believe, self-enclosed world in which even order is a manifestation of freedom.

Nor is "sacred" in this connection an altogether self-explanatory, unambiguous term. Typically, poetic play derives its sanctity, such as it is, from the higher purpose or a communal myth which it helps to articulate or enact, in its capacity as

[1] *Homo Ludens* (Boston, 1950), p. 122. [2] *Ibid.*, p. 8.

16

an integral part of a religious ritual, or as a vehicle of a social or national ideal. Yet if it is permissible to extend the word "sacred" beyond the strictly ideological realm, Huizinga's phrase may, in addition, suggest an apotheosis of play as an autonomous activity, an affirmation of its humanizing, indeed liberating impact.

I submit that considerations such as these may have some relevance to the problem which I propose to explore here—that of the images of the poet in the work of Aleksandr Pushkin. I am using the plural—"images" rather than "image"—advisedly. One of the most striking characteristics of the vast body of Pushkin's work which is directly or indirectly concerned with the theme of poetic creation is a baffling plethora of divergent, indeed often incompatible, images, concepts, personae. Jakobson and Tomashevskii[3] repeatedly call attention to the protean nature of Pushkin's vision which shuns consistency and steadfastly eludes the attempt at single interpretation on the part of the axe-grinding critic, be it Dostoevsky's myth of Pushkin as the standard-bearer of Christian humility, or the official Soviet pundit's more pedestrian effort to turn the great poet into a staunch champion of social progress. "Each image of Pushkin," says Jakobson in a provocative introduction to the selected works of Pushkin in Czech, "is so elastically ambiguous that it can be easily fitted into the most diverse contexts."[4] In terms of Isaiah Berlin's now famous dichotomy, Pushkin was a fox par excellence.[5]

Nowhere is this multiplicity of the points of view as much in evidence as it is with regard to the Pushkin image of the creator. Pushkin's metapoetry, to use a recent addition to our critical vocabulary, coined to designate a body of poetry specifically and explicitly concerned with itself, nearly exhausts

---

[3] *Vybrane spisy A. S. Puškina*, ed. A. Bem and R. Jakobson (Prague, 1936); Boris Tomashevskii, *Pushkin* (Moscow, 1925).

[4] *Ibid.*

[5] *The Hedgehog and the Fox* (New York, 1953).

the range of concepts of the poet available in the early nineteenth century. The poet in Pushkin is now a fire-eating biblical prophet, now a cool and aloof priest of pure beauty, now an impassioned bard, now a mere resonator, an all-encompassing, chameleonlike or, if one will, "Keatsian" sensibility. At the risk of sounding very obvious to a student of Russian literature I will have to consider briefly some of the highlights of Pushkin's "poet"-cycle, contained within the years 1826 to 1830, notably "The Poet" (1827), "The Prophet" (1826), "The Mob" (1828), and "To the Poet" (1830).

In the famous 1827 lyric, "The Poet," where the classicist tenor of the opening lines "as long as Apollo does not summon the poet to the holy sacrifice," coexists in a truly Pushkinian fashion with a Romantic description of the creative process ("full of sounds and turmoil"), Shelley's eulogy of the poet as a superior being is significantly modified. The poem postulates a cleavage between the poet as a man and the poet as creator, between long arid stretches of meaningless existence and the blessed moments of inspiration. Not until Apollo's summons rouses the poet from his "cold torpor" does he become transfigured and thus worthy of his calling. Leaving behind the milling crowds, he flees "wild and stern" into the solitude of "desolate waves and vastly rustling forests" to commune with his Muse and nature.

The notion of inspiration as a process triggered by a "divine call" is writ large in another famous lyric of Pushkin's, "The Prophet" (1826); only this time the role of Apollo is assumed by Jehovah. The powerfully sustained biblical imagery lends the quality of rhetorical vehemence to the portrayal of the poet's spiritual transformation. "The six-winged seraph" whom the protagonist encounters in the "gloom of the unpeopled waste,"

wrung from my mouth my sinful tongue . . . and the wise serpent's tongue he placed / between my lips with hand blood-dabbled, / and with the sword he clove my breast; / plucked out the heart he made beat higher / and in my striken bosom pressed / instead the coals of living fire.[6]

There is, however, an essential difference between the two situations. The poet who does Apollo's bidding, promptly flees the company of men to sing in proud solitude. The "I" of "The Prophet" is enjoined to turn the fire which now burns in his heart upon the souls of men:

> Arise, oh prophet, watch and hearken,
> And with my Will thy soul engird,
> Roam the great seas, the roads that darken
> And burn men's hearts with this, my Word.[7]

An orthodox formalist will see this stern sense of public responsibility and of spiritual leadership, simply as a corollary of a primary stylistic choice: the value-pattern embodied in the imagery of "The Prophet," notably, ancient Hebrew ethos, leaves little room for aesthetic individualism. Conversely, a critic of a different persuasion may argue that biblical symbolism serves here as the most appropriate "objective correlative" available within the Judaeo-Christian tradition for the stance of a moral guide, a stern monitor of sinful but redeemable mankind.

Be that as it may, the note of aristocratic aloofness from

---

[6]   И вырвал грешный мой язык,
И празднословный, и лукавый,
И жало мудрыя змеи
В уста замершие мои
Вложил десницею кровавой.
И он мне грудь рассек мечом
И сердце трепетное вынул,
И угль, пылающий огнем,
Во грудь отверстую водвинул.
                    (A. S. Pushkin, *Sochineniia* [Moscow, 1954], I, 223–24.)

[7]   Восстань, пророк, и виждь, и внемли,
Исполнись волею моей
И, обходя моря и земли,
Глаголом жги сердца людей.
                                        (*Ibid.*, p. 224.)

the *profanum vulgus* recurs in two other major landmarks of
Pushkin's metapoetry—the carefully wrought sonnet "To the
Poet" and, with polemical vengeance, in "The Mob" couched
in the form of a dialogue between the poet and the crowd. The
sonnet urges the poet to stand alone ("thou are a king and
kings must live alone") and to turn an equally deaf ear on
the plaudits and the abuse of the uninitiated multitudes. It
insists on the true artist's "inner-directedness," on his spiritual
intransigence and self-sufficiency. ("Tis thou that art the
judge, / and thine the strictest judgment of them all.")

In "The Mob" the poet lashes out against the "obtuse
crowd" which deplores the alleged uselessness of the poet's
song and urges him to harness his talent to constructive criticism by castigating vice, improving mores, and providing edification. This tiresome harangue provokes a stinging rebuke:
"What have I, a peaceful poet, to do with you?" The priest
of beauty will not descend to the level of a moral street sweeper.
The angry rhetoric subsides into the much-quoted mellifluous
finale, where soft, caressing consonants point up the "above-
the-battle" quietism of the message:

> Not for the sake of turmoil worldly,
>   For profits, or for bitter strife,
> We are born to live by inspiration,
>   We are born for prayers and sweet sounds.[8]

We may note that only three years separate this by-now-clas-
sical statement of the pure-art doctrine from the stirring lines
"Arise, oh prophet, watch and hearken / . . . and burn men's
hearts with this, my Word."

One can only sympathize with the predicament of the official

---

[8]   Не для житейского волненья,
       Не для корысти, не для битв,
       Мы рождены для вдохновенья,
       Для звуков сладких и молитв.

(Ibid., p. 260.)

Soviet literary scholar who in his effort to make Pushkin safe for Socialist realism must do his level best to try to explain away the last stanza of " The Mob." Pushkin's rejection of the utilitarian approach to art, so goes the argument, is due to the " upper-class," reactionary nature of the " crowd " which formulates the program. Presumably, Pushkin would have responded with enthusiasm to a clamor for a positive message had it come from the masses rather than from aristocratic snobs.[9] Now it is an incontrovertible fact of Pushkin's biography that the " mob " which obtruded upon the poet's privacy, which harassed him by petty sniping and malicious gossip and finally hounded him to death was the St. Petersburg high society, the courtier sycophants of an autocratic regime. This is, however, more directly relevant to the genesis of the poem under discussion than to its fundamental import. There is nothing specifically upper-class about the priggishly self-deprecatory harangue of the mob nor is there anything in the poet's rebuttal that would not be applicable to lower-class social utilitarianism. (In fact, in accusing his unsolicited advisers of preferring the " useful " kitchen pot to Phidias' " useless " statue of Apollo, Pushkin happened to anticipate the dictum of the most vocal spokesman of radical Russian criticism of the 1860's, D. Pisarev: " Boots are more important than Shakespeare!.")

Yet the champions of the art-for-art's-sake doctrine should not have rejoiced prematurely. The author of *Eugene Onegin* had a disconcerting knack for providing pithy statements of positions held halfheartedly or intermittently, if at all. Eight years later in a proudly self-assertive " The Monument " in which taking his cue from " *Exegi Monumentum*," and more directly from the eighteenth-century Russian paraphrase of Horace, Pushkin listed among his claims to distinction and posthumous fame the fact that " Kindly sentiments / I stirred by my lyre," that " in my cruel age I celebrated freedom / and

[9] A recent example of this tendency is provided by B. Meilakh's *Pushkin and His Era* [*Pushkin i ego epokha*] (Moscow, 1958).

called for ruth to those cast down." The last two lines of this passage have direct relevance to a specific aspect of Pushkin's record. It is only natural that in a poem taking stock of his total achievement Pushkin should have felt the need to acknowledge, indeed point with some pride and affection to, the libertarian strain in his work and his residual loyalty to the memories and hopes of his "Decembrist" youth. Yet the preceeding "kindly sentiments / I stirred by my lyre" has the ring of a civic cliché which one would least expect of the author of "The Mob." (Incidentally, Pushkin was not afraid of occasional banality. He knew he could absorb it.) In fact, it is not altogether inaccurate to say that in this reference to "noble sentiments," which he was allegedly helping promote, the great poet was congratulating himself on having done precisely what his *alter ego* in the 1828 lyric scornfully refused to do.

Is Pushkin, as a distinguished scholar once surmised,[10] speaking here tongue-in-cheek? Is he talking down to the generations yet unborn by pointing up those aspects of his poetic career which will more likely be appreciated by the people, than by that "most competent judge of them all, the exacting artist?" Or is this simply another instance of Pushkin's magnificent inconsistency?

Probably the latter. Pushkin's uncanny hospitality to ideas, however disparate or incompatible, strongly suggests that there is something exploratory, tentative, indeed playful about his attitude toward extant aesthetic and philosophical commitments. Not infrequently he seems to toy with ideas, to try them for size, to sound them off, as it were, without identifying himself firmly or definitively with the position thus articulated, though often felicity of phrasing produces an illusion of finality. It is as if he were reaching for the optimum verbal correlative of, or the most appropriate poetic response to, an ideational stimulus. Thus, Boris Tomashevskii could argue in his early

---

[10] In his collection of essays, *Pushkin's Wisdom* [*Mudrost' Pushkina*] (Moscow, 1919), Mikhail Gershenzon detects a note of sarcasm in the much touted civic line.

study [11] with much justification that for Pushkin each concept within his purview was primarily a poetic theme to be evaluated in terms of its aesthetic potentialities. One is often tempted to take at its face value the self-image reflected in another metapoetic lyric, "Echo," where the poet is likened to an echo, responding with perfect impartiality to any and all sounds, be they the howling of a beast, the rumble of thunder, or a girl's distant singing.

Yet to accept this simile as the answer would be to become involved with another half- or quarter-truth. For one thing, the echo or "resonator" image is only one of the many concepts of the poet encompassed by Pushkin's vision. For another, this notion suggests much too passive an attitude to the outside world to provide an adequate account of the actual workings of the poetic imagination.

Moreover, pluralism is not incompatible with involvement, be it a transient or intermittent one. When all is said and done, the cumulative effect produced by much of Pushkin's metapoetry is not one of an ideational grab-bag, of indiscriminate eclecticism, but rather of a seesaw alternation between two eloquently articulated positions, two sets of attitudes. This antinomy could often be considered as a structural feature of the Pushkin canon, for it helps determine the tenor and manner of his poetry—lyrical and narrative alike.

2.

Pushkin's earlier verses are dominated by a tug-of-war between two opposite self-images, both of which were inherited from neo-classicist poetics—the Anacreontic and the heroic ones. The dichotomy of the public versus the private, the tender versus the martial is clearly stated in the poem "Ana-

[11] *Pushkin* (Moscow, 1925).

creon's Grave," which says of the Greek master in a direct paraphrase from an Anacreontic ode: "Here placing his hands upon his lyre and gravely furrowing his brow, he wants to sing the god of battles, but all he can sing is love."

Throughout much of his Lyceum period, Pushkin seems to pattern himself after Anacreon or a more recent model, an elegantly sensuous late-classicist Batiushkov, whom the young poet described in an 1814 epistle as a " serene philosopher and poet / a happy and indolent Parnassian / a favorite of Charites." The prime emphasis here is on a quietly hedonistic enjoyment of life, on civilized leisure and emotional privacy. The poet who knows his business withdraws from the rigors and responsibilities of the life of action, leaves behind the clatter of the market place and the futile scrambling for power and fame, to sing, *procul negotiis*, the delights of love and friendship to his like-minded intimates.

The higher road of classicism, the road of seriousness and stilted grandiloquence is spurned and ridiculed while the Batiushkov-like image holds sway. Yet even in his early days Pushkin was not immune to the temptations and challenges of the heroic genre. He paid it his due first in his juvenile "Remembrances in Tsarskoe Selo," full of conventional patriotic fervor, and a few years later, more meaningfully, in a series of political poems starting with an ode "Liberty" (Volnost'). (The contrast between two contending attitudes is often reflected in the choice of genre. The Anacreontic stance encourages the use of the epistle, with its intimate, casual, often bantering tone. The poet's public emotions, e. g., moral indignation and civic scorn, find a natural outlet in an ode.)

The preamble to "Liberty" dramatizes the tension between, and the alternation of, the two images of the poet—the tender and the heroic ones. In a self-conscious and partly self-critical, gesture the poet repudiates the "wrong" Muse in order to usher in the "right" one:

Flee, vanish from my sight
    You weak queen of Cythera!
Where art thou, terror of kings,
    Proud singer of freedom? [12]

It is as if the poet felt unworthy of assuming his public role
without first casting out Venus and exorcizing the spirit of
Anacreontic frivolity.   It is as if he were announcing to the
reader who might have met him previously in another capacity: " This time I'm in dead earnest."

Chased away from a civic ode, the Anacreontic image of the
" indolent Parnassian " made its way into Pushkin's first narrative poem, "Ruslan and Ludmila." This eclectic piece of
whimsy which combines the elements of a mock epic with those
of a fairy tale opens with a characteristically nonchalant *envoi*:

For you, queens of my soul
    My beauties, for you alone
Did I jot down in the hours of golden leisure
    The preposterous tales of olden times.

        .   .   .   .

My only hope is that a maiden
    May with a quiver of love
Glance surreptitiously at my wicked poems. [13]

---

[12]   Беги, сокройся от очей,
Цитеры слабая царица!
Где ты, где ты, гроза царей,
Свободы гордая певица?   (Pushkin, *Sochineniia*, I, 106.)
[13]   Для вас, души моей царицы,
Красавицы, для вас одних
Времен минувших небылицы,
В часы досугов золотых,
Под шепот старины болтливой
Рукою верной я писал;

        .   .   .   .

Счастлив уж я надеждой сладкой,
Что дева с трепетом любви
Посмотрит, может, быть, украдкой
На песни грешные мои.   (Pushkin, *Sochineniia*, II, 16.)

This studied casualness defines the narrative tone of the poem. In the preamble to *The Igor Tale* the anonymous author eloquently insists on the authenticity of the events he is going to relate. The trademark of the narrator in "Ruslan and Ludmila" is a slightly affected pride in the irrelevance of his yarn, the pose of singing in order to while the time away, *pour le bonheur des dames.* This illusion is maintained throughout the poem in frivolous or ironical digressions. The author's periodical spell-breaking intrusions are part and parcel of Pushkin's mock-epic manner, of his irreverent tampering with the high classicist canon. At the same time this playful manner, more akin, as the poet himself remarks, to Parny's *poésie fugitive* than to Homer's heroic epic, reinforces the mundane strain in the poem and helps to keep alive the image of the author as an "infatuated chatterer" who has nothing important to say and no abiding interest in his tale and who keeps resuming it at the express request of his "tender friend." In fact, the private quality of the poet's concern is closely bound up here with a highly restricted image of the audience. The denial of the public relevance and of the essential seriousness of the poet's business leads to reducing his audience to a few "beauties," if indeed not a single love object.

The chatty intimacy of tone, the pretense of casually dashing off one's verses for the benefit of a small group of initiates constitutes one of the strands in the elusive image of the author in Pushkin's masterpiece *Eugene Onegin.* In the dedication addressed to a friendly literary historian, Pletnëv, the poem is described as a "batch of gaudy chapters, . . . a casual fruit of my amusements, insomnia, light inspirations," etc. The continuity with the manner of "Ruslan and Ludmila" is unmistakably established at the beginning of the first canto; the readers to whom the hero is being introduced are apostrophied as "friends of Ludmila and Ruslan." The import of this is clear: the new poem is ostensibly addressed to the audience with whom the poet had already established personal and aes-

thetic rapport—a select group of friends who can be expected
to be cognizant of the poet's literary mannerisms and personal
vicissitudes. Hence, the autobiographical winks at the reader,
the pseudo-cryptic hints at the author's political predicament:
" I used to roam around there [in St. Petersburg] myself / But
the North is bad for my health. . . ."

Yet the dichotomy of the private versus the public is not
always a matter of a hard-and-fast choice. There is in the
Pushkin canon at least one significant poem which, to my mind,
represents something of a borderline case, pointing as it does
to a *sui generis* nature of the poet's political commitment. I
am referring to " Arion " (1827), a lyric which hints very
broadly at Pushkin's precarious personal situation after the
brutal suppression of the Decembrist movement, in 1825:

> We numbered many in the ship,
> Some spread the sails, some pulled together
> The mighty oars; 'twas placid weather,
> The rudder in his steady grip
> Our helmsman silently was steering
> The heavy galley through the sea
> While I from doubts and sorrows free,
> Sang to the crew. When suddenly,
> A storm! And the white sea was reeling.
> The helmsman and the crew were lost
> The sailor by the storm was tossed
> Ashore but I who had been singing
> I chant the songs I loved of yore
> And on a sunned and rocky shore
> I dry my robes, all wet and clinging.[14]

---

[14] Арион
Нас было много на челне;
Иные парус напрягали,
Другие дружно упирали
Вглубь мощны весла. В тишине
На руль склонясь, наш кормщик умный

Not unnaturally the bulk of the extant commentary has focussed on the biographical implications of the poem, on its place in that interplay between realistic adjustment and emotional fidelity to the past which defined Pushkin's attitude in the post-1825 period. Viewed in this light, " Arion " was bound to be read as a fairly straightforward acknowledgment of the author's past affinity for, and association with, the Decembrist conspiracy—" *We* numbered many in the ship " was tantamount to admitting that, to use the American conversational metaphor, Pushkin and Decembrists were in the same boat— and of his continuing loyalty to the libertarian ideal ("I chant the songs I loved of yore ") , and thus bracketed together with such poems as the brave and stirring " Message to Siberia " (1828) .

Now this interpretation is valid as far as it goes. Yet the legitimate emphasis on the first person plural " we " should not blind us to the perceptible difference, if not cleavage, between the " I " of the poem and the " others," a difference which concerns both the initial function and the ultimate fate of the poet and of the crew, respectively. The imagery of the opening lines strongly suggests a division of labor as between the strong and silent men of action ("Our helmsman *silently* was steering") responsible for manning and steering the ship, and their poetic fellow traveler, if I may use nonpejoratively this tainted term, who " from doubts and sorrows free, / sang to the crew." Subsequently, when the hour of reckoning comes, it is the " others "

В молчанье правил грузный челн;
А я—беспечной веры полн—
Пловцам я пел . . . Вдруг лоно волн
Измял с налету вихорь шумный . . .
Погиб и кормщик и пловец!
Лишь я, таинственный певец,
На берег выброшен грозою,
Я гимны прежние пою
И ризу влажную мою
Сушу на солнце под скалою.

(Pushkin, *Sochineniia*, I, 232.)

that have to pay the ultimate price for their total engagement. To be sure, the lot of the shipwrecked poet tossed by the storm onto a rocky shore is not an enviable one. Yet he alone manages to survive the holocaust and is now clearly on his way to recovery.

Was the singer favored by fate because he was a poet? Was he spared in deference to the precious gift which he carried within himself? This may well be the import of the Greek myth about the poet's miraculous rescue which provided the basis for the title of the poem. Yet the tenor of the closing lines is scarcely that of rejoicing over one's good fortune. What I think I detect here is a vaguely apologetic note, a sense of embarrassment or shame, if not of actual guilt, over having gone scot free, over having escaped the grim price of death or exile exacted from the poet's fully committed travel companions. The singer's luck seems to be closely bound up with the part-time, lightweight quality of his involvement. It is not quite clear whether he survived because the Gods valued him so highly or because men—that is, society or history—did not take him too seriously. For he remains an outsider in the realm of action where serious, careworn men take upon themselves the grim but noble burden of responsibility and pay the full cost.

I am reminded of a poem by Heinrich Heine, another man of talent, if not of genius, who shuttled in his own way between the Anacreontic and the heroic planes. In the prologue to a lyrical cycle " A New Spring " (*Neuer Frühling*) Heine used a somewhat conventional image of a fully armed warrior hamstrung by cupids to convey a sense of guilt about his poetic self-indulgence:

> In Gemälde-Galerien
> Siehst du oft das Bild des Manns,
> Der zum Kampfe wollte ziehen,
> Wohlbewehrt mit Schild und Lanz'.

> Doch ihn necken Amoretten,
> Rauben Lanze ihm und Schwert,
> Binden ihn mit Blumenketten,
> Wie er auch sich mürrisch wehrt.
> So in holden Hindernissen
> Wind' ich mich mit Lust und Leid,
> Während andre kämpfen müssen
> In dem grossen Kampf der Zeit.[15]

The rough English approximation of the last stanza would read: "Thus amidst alluring handicaps, I grapple with pleasure and pain while the others must fight in the great battle of the age."

Here was a sentiment characteristic of, if not necessarily unique to, the nineteenth century. It was an age which aroused in the literary man strong and often contradictory feelings. To Matthew Arnold (as interpreted by Lionel Trilling) it appeared as "moving and profound" and at the same time "deeply unpoetical."[16] It was unpoetical or it was likely to so impress a nostalgic poet because it often seemed to lack in grace, elegance and glamour. Yet it was moving and profound because the drama of national awakening and free-swinging social conflict had a powerful claim on the moral sensitivity and imagination of the literary artist. An aroused social conscience, a keen if intermittent awareness of what Keats called "the giant agony of the world,"[17] was bound to activate a latent uneasiness, a vague sense of guilt over the *licentia poetica*, that is, the poet's privilege to indulge in the luxuries of "impulse, pleasure and imagination,"[18] and to that extent to withdraw from the realm of public responsibility, desert the battlefield.

Yet, to return to Pushkin and Heine, beyond a certain point

---

[15] Heinrich Heine, *Sämtliche Werke* (Leipzig, 1920), I, 203.

[16] *Matthew Arnold* (New York, 1955), p. 25.

[17] John Keats, "The Fall of Hyperion," *Complete Poems and Selected Letters* (New York, 1935).

[18] Lionel Trilling, *The Opposing Self* (New York, 1959), p. xiii.

analogy breaks down. Not only was Heine in actuality more heavily and frequently committed than was Pushkin, but, and perhaps more importantly, the "engagement" loomed large in the image of himself which he was seeking to project. Though he is remembered today more for his charming and whimsical lyrics than for his pungent, but often topical, polemics, he apparently wanted to be revered by posterity primarily as a fighter: "I do not know," he said shortly before his death, "if I deserve that a laurel wreath should once be laid on my coffin. Poetry, dearly as I have loved it, has always been to me but a divine plaything. I have never attached any great value to poetical fame. But lay on my coffin a sword for I was a brave soldier in the liberation war of humanity." [19]

Heine's disclaimer of any interest in poetical fame clearly is to be taken no more seriously than was Chekhov's frequent insistence that literature was simply his favorite hobby. Yet if this was in part a pose, it was the kind of posturing that was utterly alien to Pushkin. While his image of himself as a poet varied from poem to poem and from mood to mood, his self-definition was always inseparable from his poetic calling. Solemn or frivolous, proud or vaguely apologetic, a bard or a troubadour, he was always first and foremost a poet wedded to his lyre for better or worse. Though the sincerity of his transient or alternating ideological involvements cannot be gainsaid, it is poetry which had his primary allegiance, it is the free play of the creative imagination which was the focus of his sturdiest beliefs.

3.

The nature of this overriding commitment emerges most fully from Pushkin's last extended pronouncement on the poet and poetry—"Egyptian Nights" (1835), an unfinished prose

[19] Quoted in *Poetry and Prose*, ed. J. Bryson (Cambridge, Mass., 1954), p. 395.

narrative which toward the end shades off into verse and which contains one of the gems of Pushkin's metapoetry. As Ralph Matlaw recently pointed out,[20] the image of the poet in "Egyptian Nights" is split up into Charskii, a dedicated artist who poses as a blasé dandy, and an itinerant Italian improviser who turns out verses at request before snobbish and uncomprehending audiences. The two protagonists represent disparate, indeed opposite, facets of the late Pushkin's ambiguous predicament and creative personality. Charskii is in a sense a throwback to the hero of "The Poet," who shuttles between the mundane triviality of everyday life and rare moments of poetic ecstasy. This time, however, the worldliness is not so much a human, all too human, weakness, but a mode of self-preservation, a mask which keeps the fools and idlers at bay and thus helps the poet salvage his social standing (clearly jeopardized by the reputation of a mere scribbler), and more importantly, his spiritual and creative privacy. Thus Charskii embodies in a more extreme, and outwardly more successful, form Pushkin's embattled class pride and his severely taxed sense of personal dignity. Conversely, the Italian "wandering juggler" who combines the divine spark with meretricious cunning and a thoroughly unpoetical greed is a shabby caricature of the author's often humiliating financial dependence on the approval of the *profanum vulgus.*

Yet the juxtaposition of the Russian gentleman-poet and the Italian virtuoso, as well as the symbiotic relationship which prevails between them, has implications beyond the poet's social status. The uncanny facility of the improviser who by a sleight-of-hand turns into ringing poetry any subject, any theme big or small suggested by his audience, may well stand for the echo or resonator aspect of Pushkin's poetic genius, for his allegedly unselective responsiveness to external stimuli, and

[20] " Poetry and the Poet in Romantic Society as Reflected in Pushkin's *The Egyptian Nights*," *The Slavonic and East European Review,* XXXIII, No. 80 (December, 1954), 102–19.

more broadly, for the notion of poetry as magic, as a virtuoso stunt, a dazzling display of craftsmanship. By the same token, Charskii's stance may well epitomize the hard core of conviction and dedication behind the protective cover of worldly frivolity. This becomes especially apparent in the telling scene where Charskii, in testing the foreigner's prowess, suggests as a topic for his improvisation the notion that, "The poet himself chooses the subject of his verse; the crowd has no right to command his inspiration." The poem triggered by this suggestion is perhaps the most ringing declaration of the poet's independence to be found in Pushkin's legacy.

"The poet comes: His eyes are open, but he sees no one." A passer-by takes him to task for wandering aimlessly and looking downward instead of aspiring to heaven. "A true poet is obliged to choose a lofty subject for an inspired song." The poet counters this tedious lecture by reaffirming the principle "*Spiritus flat ubi vult,*" in a string of similes. Like a wind uselessly swirling in a ravine, while a ship avidly awaits its life-giving breath, like an eagle leaving the mountain peaks only to land on a measly stump, like young Desdemona in love with her Moor, the poetic inspiration is unfathomable, unpredictable, unaccountable for, in short, it is free.

On the face of it, the position of the passer-by seems to be the reverse of that taken by the obtuse mob in the 1828 lyric. The latter, we will recall, is trying to drag the poet down to trivial and undignified didactic chores, while the former bids the creator to look heavenward. Yet in either case the unsolicited advice is spurned and properly so. Clearly what is repudiated here is not a specific program or set of demands urged upon the creator, but any and all social pressures, any and all forms of outside dictation, externally imposed dogmas, preconceptions, taboos, constraints. What is asserted is the fundamentally Romantic tenet that inspiration has laws of its own which do not yield to fiats or prohibitions and are not susceptible of rational analysis. The demands which the poet in turn makes on the crowd are very simple indeed: it need not appreciate, let alone revere his work. All it has to do, is to leave him alone.

Autonomy of art, creative freedom—this when all is said and done is the central article of Pushkin's faith, the principal element of consistency in this magnificently inconsistent heritage, the only coherent message which emerges from Pushkin's polyphonic metapoetry. This is not to say that the only freedom Pushkin ever cared about was freedom for the artist. As every student of Russian literature knows full well, свобода (freedom) or вольность (liberty) was one of the major themes in Pushkin's work, one of the key terms in his vocabulary. From the stilted libertarian ode, through the derivative Byronic rebellion of " The Prisoner of the Caucasus," down to the stock-taking " The Monument " this watchword keeps recurring, now as an epitome of a righteous political order (Liberty), or as the fondest hope, indeed a love-object of the budding Russian intelligentsia,[21] now reaching exuberantly beyond a purely political realm as the Byronic-Rousseauist ideal of a liberation of the self from crippling societal norms.

Yet as the spectacular fluidity of the Napoleonic age was giving way to the rocklike stability of the " Holy Alliance " Europe, the more expansive concept of freedom appeared increasingly precarious. Though Pushkin never abandoned inwardly his nostalgia for the " paradise lost " of youthful idealism, he seems to have lost his faith in political liberty as an operative principle and sought to come to terms with the power realities of post-1825 Russia. In 1824, in a poem addressed to the sea, where the irrepressible element was to epitomize the stormy grandiloquence of the Byronic rebellion, he bade a wistful farewell to the Romantic view of reality as a malleable

---

[21] Consider the erotic simile in Pushkin's early political lyric " To Chaadaev ": " In hope, in torment, we are turning / Toward freedom, waiting her command / Thus anguished do young lovers stand / Who wait the promised tryst with yearning." (*The Works of Alexander Pushkin*, ed. A. Yarmolinsky [New York, 1936]).

matter, shaped largely by the will and vision of event-making personalities, as a heroic playground of the self. Now the play was over, the curtain rung down. "The world has become empty" ("To the Sea"), empty of color, dash and daring. The Iron age confined the individual within the narrow limits of a restrictive political order, of harsh material contingency. In the realm of action the somber word "fate" increasingly displaces the buoyancy and bounce of "freedom": "the *fate* of man is everywhere the same" ("To the Sea"); "And fatal passions everywhere, / and there is no escaping the Fates" ("The Gypsies"). To reverse a famous dictum of Friedrich Engels', one observes in Pushkin's middle period a shift, if not exactly a leap, from the kingdom of freedom to the kingdom of necessity.

The bureaucratic restrictions and commercial pressures of the 1830's seemed to have made social reality increasingly difficult to bear and still more difficult to change or influence. In this oppressive climate the poet's creative privacy acquires a strategic, indeed a central, value. With art turning into a spiritual oasis, an enclave of dignity and repose within the callous and unresponsive world, the dedication to creative freedom is no longer an organic part of a larger thrust toward a way of life more consonant with the demands of a creative personality. It becomes rather an embattled individual's last line of defense against the authoritarian juggernaut.

This specialized, not to say professional, variant of freedom finds characteristic expression in a lyric written a year before Pushkin's death. "From Pindemonte" (1836) come such shibboleths of liberalism as the right to vote, representative government, freedom of the press, "words, words, words." Political freedom, a hardly feasible objective in the Russia of 1836, is dubbed irrelevant as Pushkin declares himself champion of "another, better freedom": of the poet's right, "to live without giving account to anyone, to serve and please no one but oneself," a right "not to bend either one's neck or one's conscience before those in power, to wander around at will, delighting in the divine marvels of nature and quivering blissfully before the creations of the arts and inspiration. That is happiness, those are rights for you!"

It is this aspect of Pushkin's legacy which was invoked gratefully and affectionately by one of modern Russia's greatest lyrical poets, Aleksandr Blok who had just emerged from a Dionysian intoxication with the "music of the Revolution" to face the bleak reality of creeping bureaucratic tutelage over Russian letters. Blok chose the occasion of the eighty-fourth anniversary of Pushkin's death to sound a pointed warning against those officials who "set out to guide poetry along particular channels, infringing upon its secret freedom and hindering it from fulfilling its mysterious mission."[22] At the end of his memorable speech "On the Calling of the Poet" Blok proclaimed "just for fun" a few anticlimactically sober propositions, timely reminders all, of the autonomy of art and importance of craft in an era of do-it-yourself literary amateurishness, such as these: "One should not call art things which have quite different names; in order to create works of art one ought to know how to do it." He concluded: "Let us swear loyalty to these gay truths of common sense, against which we have sinned so much, by the gay name of Pushkin."[23]

Measured against Pushkin's entire career, Blok's adjective may sound somewhat misleading. It fits closely enough, to be sure, the impish wit of Pushkin's epigrams, the carefree sensuality of much of his erotic poetry, the youthful buoyance of the early cantos of *Eugene Onegin*. Yet, one may properly inquire, how about the weary resignation of "Tis time, my friend, tis time," the tragic moral realism of *The Bronze Horseman*, the somber "The Feast During the Plague," the note of despair in "May God Prevent Me From Going Mad"?

[22] A. Blok, "O naznachenii poeta," *Sochineniia* [*Works*] (Moscow, 1955), II, 347–55.
[23] *Ibid.*, p. 355.

Clearly, if "gaiety" were to mean simply "good cheer,"
Blok's phrase would be no more accurate than is the popular
notion about the Apollonian serenity of the ancient Greeks.
But the epithet "gay" can be easily sustained, if it is interpreted not in terms of the over-all stance of the man and
thinker, but in those of the poet's attitude toward his craft or,
to return to our starting point, of what Huizinga has called
"the gay abandon, mirth and jollity" inseparable from poetry
as play.

In no work of Russian literature have these qualities been
exhibited more brilliantly than the first canto of Pushkin's narrative masterpiece where within a flexible yet firm framework
of the so-called Onegin stanza the verse glitters away as it
playfully skips from subject to subject, glorying in its own
texture, exuberantly displaying its manifold potentialities. In
his later work Pushkin never recaptured fully this Mozartian
spirit of aesthetic insouciance. Yet if harassments and disen-
chantments chastened the man and often dampened his spirits,
they did not manage to destroy the poet's mirth or to impair
his unstodgy, unportentous yet firm belief in the indispensability of whimsy, the absolute essentiality of the inessential,
the high seriousness of play as an exercise in, and testimony to,
human freedom.

3. THE COST OF THE IMAGE:
THE STRANGE CASE OF ZYGMUNT KRASIŃSKI

" Le poète a une malédiction pour sa vie et une bénédiction pour son nom."

(de Vigny, " Stello ")

1.

Few students of Polish literature will deny that *The Undivine Comedy* by Zygmunt Krasiński (1812–59) is a remarkable and a baffling phenomenon. A powerfully projected vision of a social apocalypse, cast in the form of a Faustian drama, this work of a twenty-one-year-old Polish Romantic poet has several claims to distinction. Though little known abroad, *The Undivine Comedy* is without a doubt one of the most widely relevant literary creations in the language. It represents the high point of the author's achievement, indeed the only work of genius in what is increasingly recognized as a spotty and predominantly second-rate poetic career.[1] Finally, it contains the most explicit and bitter critique of the poet to be found in Polish—and not only Polish—Romantic literature.

This latter aspect of the play has been largely overshadowed by its social dimension. The bulk of the commentators have addressed themselves to the lurid scenes of the imminent showdown between aristocracy and democracy, the haves and the

---

[1] See especially, Czeslaw Miłosz, " Krasjński's Retreat," *The Polish Review,* **IV,** No. 4 (Autumn, 1959), 72–86.

have-nots, which dominate the last two acts of Krasiński's drama. Yet, as a number of Krasiński scholars (e. g., Górski, Lednicki, Kleiner), have pointed out,[2] *The Undivine Comedy* encompasses two distinct, and on the face of it, entirely divergent, themes—" the tragedy of the artist as a human being and the tragic insolubility of the social problem in the modern world." [3]

These disparate emphases are held together, within the permissive framework of a loose-jointed Romantic drama, by the unity of the chief protagonist and, more substantially perhaps, by the underlying notion of a heartless world.[4]

The warning against the moral pitfalls of poetry is sounded in no uncertain terms in the high-flown poetic prose of the preamble to part one. The aposthophe to the poet starts with a qualified apotheosis and ends in a partial indictment:

Stars above thy head and under thy feet the waves of the sea. On the sea waves a rainbow speeds before thee and rends the mist in twain. What thou seest is thine—the coast, the towns and the people are thy possessions—the sky is thine and it seems as though thy glory was unequal. Thou playeth in the ears of others inconceivable delights of melody. Thou bindeth and unbindeth the heart as though it were a garland with which thy fingers played. And what dost thou feel thyself? What dost thou create and think? *Through thee floweth a stream of beauty but thou are not beauty thyself.*

Whence come thou, empty shadow that dost witness the light, but knowest not the light thyself, neither hast seen it or perceived it? Who created thee in wrath or in irony—who gave thee thy vile life, so delusive that thou can seem an angel a moment ere thou sinkest into the mire, ere, like a reptile thou creepest into the slime and are stifled by it? . . . Not that I complain of thee, oh, poesy, mother of beauty and salvation. Only he is unhappy who in worlds

---

[2] Konrad Górski, " Stulecie ' Nieboskiej Komedji '," *Literatura a prądy umysłowe* (Warszawa, 1938); Wacław Lednicki, " The Undivine Comedy," *The Polish Review,* IV, No. 3 (Summer, 1959), 106–35; Juliusz Kleiner, introduction to a recent edition of *The Undivine Comedy* [*Nieboska Komedja*] (Wrocław, 1959).

[3] Górski, *Literatura a prądy umysłowe,* p. 205.

[4] Lednicki, " The Undivine Comedy," p. 134.

in womb, in worlds that are doomed to perish must remember or foresee thee; for thou only destroyeth those who have consecrated themselves to thee, who have become the living voices of thy glory.

Blessed is he in whom thou hast dwelt as God dwelt in the world, unseen, unheard. Such a one carries thee as a star on his brow and will not *separate himself from thy love by an abyss of words.* He will love mankind and come forth as a man among his brethren. But he who betrayeth thee too soon and delivereth thee up to the empty delights of man, thou shalt scatter a few flowers upon his head and turn away and he will play with withered flowers and all his life will weave his funeral wreath.[5]

Count Henry, the hero of *The Undivine Comedy*, clearly belongs to the "unblessed" category. Outwardly a commanding figure, he proves at closer range a moral cripple, a tragically warped human being, an empty shell. Characteristically, his inadequacy is most conclusively revealed in the early phase of the drama which is concerned with the private life of the poet.

As the drama opens, Count Henry reluctantly "descends to earthly vows." He is clearly incapable of reciprocating, indeed appreciating, the love and devotion of "a mere woman of clay and mire," his bride. Marriage appears to him as too humdrum, prosaic an undertaking. Thus, after a brief period of infatuation with his wife, he abandons her, in pursuit of a more glamorous apparition, only to recoil in horror when the romantic *femme fatale* turns out to be a hideous fiend. Urged on by "good spirits," Count Henry returns home, but he comes too late to repair the wreckage. His neglected wife is in an insane asylum and the child is crippled for life. With the relentlessness of Greek tragedy or, perhaps more relevantly, of an Ibsenian drama, the sins of fathers are visited upon the sons. In a pathetic attempt to shield her little boy from the fate which befell her, notably, losing Count Henry's love, the half-insane mother exclaims over the infant's cradle: "I curse you if you

[5] Zygmunt Krasiński, *The Undivine Comedy*, trans. Harriette E. Kennedy and Z. Umińska (London–Warsaw, 1924), pp. 1–3. [My italics.]

will not be a poet!" Ironically, it is the fulfillment of Maria's fervent prayers that turns out to be a curse—a source of isolation and physical helplessness. At the age of ten Henry's frail, hypersensitive child is struck with blindness.[6]

Thus, on the eve of the turbulent public events which will claim all the moral strength he can muster, Count Henry sadly contemplates the ruins of his private world. As he watches the helpless little dreamer, his child, he is too human not to feel remorse or anguish, yet he is not human enough—or perhaps too much of a poet—not to dramatize his lot, not to couch his anguish in sonorous poetic prose. For he is forever "composing a drama" as the mocking demon (or is it an inner voice?) reminds him at all critical junctures.

According to the testimony of Krasiński's close friend and confidant, Danielewicz, the poet initially intended to make the protagonist of *The Undivine Comedy* a consistently ineffectual, indeed a somewhat preposterous character. His private inadequacy was to spill into the realm of political action. This is how Danielewicz summarized the plot of the still emerging play in his letter to the author's imperious father, General Wincenty Krasiński: "he [Count Henry] neglects his wife and drives her to death, he causes the unhappiness of his child, and finally plays a rather comical, for a totally passive and insignificant, role amidst political events, which makes him look a bit like a clown. Though the people around him are not worth much more than the poet, it is still a step in the right direction that he [Krasiński] should have given him a tragic *bouffe* appearance."[7] The notion that the poet tends to cut a comic figure in the theater of public events, because he is oversensitive, volatile or out of touch with reality was not new in 1833 (e. g., Goethe's "Torquato Tasso"). Nor was it unat-

---

[6] Krasiński scholars have noted a significant affinity between Orcio and his creator. Krasiński himself suffered from an acute eye disease and was at some point threatened with total blindness.

[7] A letter of July 4, 1833, quoted in, J. Kallenbach, *Z. Krasiński, Życie i tworczość lat młodych* (1812-1838), 2 vol. (Lwów, 1904).

tractive to Krasiński's entourage as Danielewicz's premature gloating ("a step in the right direction") clearly indicates. The fact of the matter is, however, that the initial design was drastically modified. In the final version of *The Undivine Comedy*, Henry is the only man worthy of the name in the aristocratic camp. He towers above the craven degenerates and the slick opportunists who make up the lost generation of the once allegedly glorious and proudly elite. Though he has no illusions about the outcome of the showdown, he does not hesitate to assume leadership, and when the chips are down he chooses death rather than abject surrender. No wonder Count Henry is the only aristocrat whom Pankras, the powerful and ruthless leader of the revolutionary masses, respects and attempts to win over in what is one of the most memorable confrontations in Polish drama.

Yet neither his courage nor his feudal sense of honor can redeem Count Henry as a human being. In one of the last scenes of the drama, set symbolically in the dungeon of the Gothic castle in which Henry and his reluctant followers make their last stand, the clairvoyant child-poet Orcio hears the verdict over his father pronounced by "voices from beyond": "Because thou has loved nothing and honored nothing except thyself, thou are damned, damned forever." [8] To underscore the fact that Henry's offense is a direct consequence of his having consecrated himself to poetry, Krasiński makes his hero exclaim as he leaps from the tower of the besieged castle into the unrelieved blackness of the abyss: "Cursed be thou, oh poesy, as I am cursed for all the ages!" [9]

Clearly, Count Henry's failure is not one of will but of heart, not one of the public act but of the inner motive. His staunch defense of a lost cause was dictated less by loyalty to a principle or of a way of life than by lust for power, however short-lived, and the flair for a heroic, masterful pose. When elected

[8] Krasiński, *The Undivine Comedy*, p. 98.
[9] *Ibid.*, p. 107.

leader of an embattled patrician band, he exults thus, in a moment of splendid isolation:

How good it is to be master, a ruler—to look, through from a deathbed, upon the wills of others gathered around me, and upon you, my adversaries, plunged into an abyss and crying to me from out its depths, as the damned cry to heaven. Be that as it may, a few days remain, I shall enjoy their bliss to the full. I shall rule, I shall fight, I shall live. *This is my last song!* [10]

Characteristically, the word " song " occurs first in the scene of the wedding ball when Count Henry urges his weary bride to dance some more for him. " Oh! how lovely you are in your pallor! You are flushed with embarrassment and fatigue. Oh! endlessly, endlessly shall you be my song! " [11] It is this compulsion to stylize each experience into a " song," to dissolve each potential emotion into its verbal correlative, its equivalent poetic cliché—coupled with egotistic *hubris*—that lies at the core of Count Henry's emotional bankruptcy. "Imagination without heart is Satan himself," wrote Krasiński to his English friend and soul mate Henry Reeve on January 8, 1833, that is, shortly before plunging into *The Undivine Comedy.* "Imagination without heart," poetic fancy glorying in itself and forever "playing with withered flowers " of its own manufacture instead of reaching toward the artist's fellow humans, this is the story of Count Henry.[12] His sin and the source of his moral downfall is aesthetic narcissism which thwarts spontaneity, frustrates any meaningful human contact, destroys

[10] *Ibid.*, pp. 93–94. [My italics.]

[11] *Ibid.*, p. 5.

[12] A similar note is sounded in a much quoted passage from Krasiński's letter to Henry Reeve, dated April 14, 1833:

Il y a délices ineffables pour l'artiste; mais aussi , il est destiné à souffrir plus que tout autre dans ce monde. A la vérité, son égoisme est sublime, mais c'est toujours de l'égoisme . . . . Il ne saura jamais ce que c'est véritablement que l'amour d'une femme, car pour lui tout est lui . . . . Il aime ses chefs d'œuvres, mais il n'aime rien de l'autre . . . . Il vit au milieu des hommes comme Cain, portant une malédiction sur son front. (*Correspondance de S. Krasiński et Henry Reeve* [Paris, 1908], II, 44.)

the very possibility of love as it immures the isolated artist in the prison of his fevered self.[13]

2.

Commentaries upon the image of the poet in *The Undivine Comedy* have tended to emphasize the unique status of Krasiński's drama vis-à-vis the Romantic canon. Professor Górski maintained that Krasiński was far ahead of his time in his awareness of the moral dangers of self-dramatization, of poeticizing one's own life.[14] More recently Wacław Lednicki argued that Krasiński's " condemnation of the ' unlucky gift ' that the muses bring to man " was a major deviation from the " cult of the poet established by the Romantics," even while he qualified this assertion by admitting the relevance of the poetry-as-curse theme to such Romantic works as de Vigny's " Eloa." [15]

Actually, the matter is a bit more complex than this. That the concept of the creator as a superior being, a seer, a prophet inspired from on high, was central to Romantic poetics can hardly be denied. In such a *locus classicus* of Romantic apologetics as Shelley's " Defense of Poetry," the poets are not only " acknowledged legislators of the world," and " philosophers of the very loftiest power." They are also, much to the surprise of some poets and most Philistines, " men of the most spotless virtue, the most consummate prudence, the most fortunate of men." [16]

Yet, fortunately this is not the only extant Romantic concept of the poet. What made romanticism the fascinating and

[13] John Keats, " The Fall of Hyperion," *Complete Poems and Selected Letters* (New York, 1935), p. 386.

[14] Górski, *Literatura a prądy umysłowe*, p. 205.

[15] Lednicki, " The Undivine Comedy," p. 112.

[16] As quoted in, René Wellek, *A History of Modern Criticism, 1750–1950,* II *The Romantic Age* (New Haven, 1955), 124.

vital movement it was, was not the rhapsodic eloquence of its self-congratulation, but its inconsistencies, internal contradictions, indeed its intermittent dialectical awareness of tension, contradiction and ambivalence. The inevitable reverse side of the worship of the poet—self-criticism, self-accusation, self-debunking,—looms larger in the Romantic tradition than Górski's and Lednicki's analyses seem to allow. The poet's " otherness " was not infrequently viewed in Romantic writings both as a blessing and a curse, a source of pain, suffering and alienation as well as of bliss, ecstasy, and superior wisdom. This is not to query the fundamental soundness of the Polish scholars' insistence on the distinctiveness and the modern tenor of Krasiński's contribution. It is rather to suggest that the relative originality of Krasiński's position cannot be properly gauged without considering some other instances of Romantic self-criticism and self-doubt, and some of the assumptions underlying the Romantic ideal of the poet.[17]

A few salient test cases come to mind. The cluster of moral estrangement, destructiveness, and finally damnation which defines County Henry's predicament reminds one inescapably of Byron's *Manfred*. Indeed there is a distinctly Manfredian tinge to Count Henry's posturing and to some of the settings in part one of *The Undivine Comedy*. Not unlike Manfred's monologues, Count Henry's lonely meditations, punctured time and again by "voices from beyond " unfold against the background of somberly spectacular landscapes. These similarities need not be viewed as purely coincidental. It is an established fact that Krasiński had read and pondered *Manfred* before embarking on his masterpiece. " ' Manfred,' " he says in a

---

[17] Parenthetically, both Polish scholars are perfectly justified in urging a fundamental divergence between Krasiński's stern verdict and the critique of the poet contained in Pushkin's famous lyric " The Poet." The difference between the two concepts is obvious. The ineradicable weakness of Pushkin's poet lies in the fact that after all he is only human. The flaw in Count Henry is his not being human enough. The former is inadequate in spite of being a poet, the latter because of it.

letter to Henry Reeve, "became a favorite of mine. I have always liked the world of spirits."[18]

To be sure, Manfred is not a poet in the strict sense of the word. Yet as a Faustian personality in search of knowledge and fullness of life, as a richly endowed individual, he could be considered a Keatsian "man of genius." Whatever the label, he pays for his quest the price exacted from Count Henry by his poetic calling—that of loneliness, despair, and doom.

"And a magic voice and verse / hath baptized thee with a curse . . . ," "A blighted trunk upon a cursed tree," ". . . My embrace was fatal," "My joys, my griefs, my passions and my powers / made me a stranger. Though I wore the form / I had no sympathy with breathing flesh . . . ,"[19] could not all these lines, and some others, be applied, without any editorial tampering, to the hapless husband of Maria and father of Orcio, to the embattled defender of the Castle of the Holy Trinity?

Yet the resemblance, however striking, is a partial one. The similarities of rhetoric and decor should not blind us to the essential differences in moral tenor and perspective. While self-reference is apparent in both instances,[20] only in Krasiński do we find anguish and a sense of guilt, a genuine rejection of that part of oneself embodied in the hero. Where Krasiński laments his moral alienation, Byron glories in it. In the Byronic tale of woe there is punishment—meted out by the outside world—but there is really no crime, except the original sin committed by society against the hero. Where the richly endowed individual is proclaimed a measure of all things and a source of all values,[21] it is always the others that are to blame for his moral

---

[18] Quoted in, Kallenbach, Z. *Krasiński*, I, 230.

[19] "Manfred," *The Complete Poetical Works of Byron* (Boston, 1933), pp. 481, 486.

[20] As Krasiński's correspondence with Henry Reeve clearly indicates, the author of *The Undivine Comedy* was not immune to the weaknesses which he excoriates in Count Henry, e. g., egotism, an urge toward self-dramatization, and an ultra-romantic view of marriage.

[21] In an illuminating discussion of the romantic world-view, George H. Mead

transgression. (Even a collusion with the Devil can be viewed
as forced upon the hero by the stifling hypocrisy of official
ethics.) Though the curse which weighs upon Manfred is ultimately destructive both of his life and of the happiness of
those around him, it becomes another badge of distinction,
another proof of his superiority to the common herd. Byron's
satanism is simply a narcissism *à rebours*, a form of moral
dandyism if not another Byronic pose. To put it in less loaded
terms, it is a mode of Prometheian challenge to conventional
morality where evil is flaunted in defiance of the accepted and
presumably meaningless notion of goodness.

Krasiński's position is fundamentally different. When he
hauls Count Henry to court, and a part of himself, the verdict
which is to follow is informed by an ethical code which ante-
dates, and is at variance with, the self-oriented Byronic rebellion—the Christian gospel of love and grace.

To be sure, English romanticism can boast a more serious
attempt to confront the problem of the poet's human inadequacy, or to use F. Kermode's apposite phrase, of "the cost of
the image."[22] Indeed, after Trilling's and Kermode's illuminating essays[23] it is difficult to ignore, in any discussion of the
nineteenth-century poet's growing self-awareness, the contribution of John Keats.

Keats saw more clearly than did most of his contemporaries
the price of poetry's unique delights. While the normal man,
he says in "The Fall of Hyperion" "knows the pain alone,
the joy alone, distinct," "the dreamer [read "poet"] venoms
all his days, bearing more woe than all his sins deserve."
Another passage of the same poem asserts the moral superiority

---

says among other things; "We come back to the existence of the self as a primary
fact. That is what we exist upon. That is what gives the standard to values. In
this situation the self puts itself forward as the ultimate reality." (*Movements of
Thought in The Nineteenth Century* [Chicago, 1936], pp. 61–62.)

[22] Frank Kermode, *The Romantic Image* (New York, 1957), p. 8.

[23] Lionel Trilling, "The Poet as Hero: Keats in His Letters," *The Opposing Self*
(New York, 1959), pp. 3–49; Kermode, *The Romantic Image*, especially pp. 7–10.

of a man of action who feels " the giant agony of the world " and seeks to alleviate it vis-à-vis the self-immured visionary, a mere " dreaming thing." [24]

And then, to be sure, there is Keats's much cited complaint about the threat which poetic calling presents to the coherence of the poet's self: " Men of genius," he wrote in his letter to Benjamin Bailey [as distingushed from " men of power " who have " a proper self "] " have not any individuality, any determined character." [25] Nearly a year later he elaborated thus:

> As for poetical character itself it is not itself . . . it has no self—it is everything and nothing—it has no character—it enjoys light and shade. It does as much delight in conceiving Iago as in Imogen. A poet is the most unpoetical of anything in existence, because he has no identity—he is continually . . . filling some other Body—the Sun, the Moon, the Sea, and Men and Women who are creatures of impulse are poetical and have about them an unchangeable attribute, the poet has none, no identity—he is certainly the most unpoetical of all God's creatures.[26]

The last sentence bears remarkable resemblance to Krasiński's memorable line " Through thee floweth a stream of beauty, but thou art not beauty thyself." Both phrases insist upon a cleavage, indeed a contrast between the *artifex* and the artifact, between the nature of the poem and the nature of the poet. Keats and Krasiński seem to be agreed that, ironically enough, the creator of things of beauty is a very unbeautiful thing to behold.

Yet once again the analogy should not be pushed too far. There is a discernible difference of tone between the two statements: where Krasiński is anguished, Keats is baffled and, if one will, annoyed. The discrepancy is quite proper, for, despite the appearances, Krasiński and Keats are not saying the same thing. As the nature of Count Henry's moral failure clearly

[24] Keats, " The Fall of Hyperion," pp. 385–86.
[25] *The Selected Letters of John Keats* (New York, 1956), p. 98.
[26] *Ibid.*, p. 166. [My italics.]

suggests, the meaning of the key term "beauty" in Krasiński's line does double service: it shifts subtly from the aesthetic to the ethical plane. What is implied here is that the dedication to poetry, as interpreted by Count Henry, robs the poet of an essential human quality, of his potential for love and goodness, i. e., for spiritual beauty: in his search for glamour Count Henry forfeits his chance of becoming an inwardly, i. e., truly beautiful person. Conversely, when Keats maintains that the poet is an unpoetical creature he means not that he is morally objectionable or ugly, but that he is shapeless, amorphous, fluid. The lack which the English poet bemoans is not one of integrity but of integration, of unity or better still, form, that is, precisely of that quality which lies at the root of the unique effect achieved by the poem.[27] Thus, even while fluidity of personality, absence of the discernible ego structure, can be viewed as a moral problem, it is not altogether inaccurate to say that whenever Keats deplores the poet's predicament, he does so on predominantly aesthetic grounds; Krasiński laments it on thoroughly ethical ones.[28]

3.

It may be obvious by now that Krasiński did inject a distinctive note into the Romantic chorus of self-adulation and occa-

[27] The above distinction may have been suggested by an observation of Lionel Trilling's. He says in describing Arnold's attitude toward the nineteenth century: "It is no easy task, Matthew Arnold is willing to concede, to be a poet in the nineteenth century. It is an age which, though moving and profound, he finds deeply unpoetical, not because it is ugly but because it is without unity." (*Matthew Arnold* [New York, 1955], p. 25).

[28] It is interesting to note that in his correspondence Krasiński at times sounds more "Keatsian" than he does in *The Undivine Comedy*. "What does it mean," he groaned once in a letter to his father, "that allegedly I understand everybody while nobody understands me? Does not this mean that I am not an individual, that I have no character of my own, but just an overdeveloped nervous and moral susceptibility like a woman's, which enables me be it for a while, to get into anybody's feelings?" (Quoted by Kallenbach, Z. *Krasiński*, II, 176).

sional self-debunking. The above casual juxtapositions, and there could be others, tell only part of the story. The complex relationship between Krasiński's self-criticism and the Romantic mythology of the poet cannot be reduced to partial analogies between his impassioned harangue and the *dicta* of some of his illustrious contemporaries. However drastically may the view of the poet held by Krasiński diverge from the mainstream of the Romantic tradition, it cannot be understood, indeed apprehended, outside of the Romantic context. Not only is the principal target of Krasiński's attack—the pitfalls of self-dramatization—a recognizably Romantic fallacy, but, more importantly, as Kleiner and Weintraub have properly insisted,[29] the line of attack, the terms of indictment, are part and parcel of the *Zeitgeist*. To put it differently, Krasiński's case against the false poet is both a challenge to the Romantic idolatry of the creator and its direct corollary.

It is hardly necessary to insist upon an organic connection between an extravagant self-assertion and occasional self-disparagement or self-digust. Where no actual performance, however impressive, can ever live up to the extravagant expectations aroused by the idealized image, disenchantment and spiritual hangover are bound to occur intermittently, if not regularly. But the matter does not end here. The Romantic view of poetic creation as a storehouse of "the very loftiest" wisdom, a gateway to the truth, or, in Krasiński's words, "mother of salvation," led paradoxically but inexorably to the tendency to demean, and cavil at, poetry as a literary craft.

Romantic poetics postulates a cleavage between the poet and the outside world. Within this framework, poetry is no longer a matter primarily of "making" things of beauty, of purveying delight or uplift to a society whose purposes the "maker" accepts or takes for granted. In an allegedly vulgar, Philistine, and insensitive world the poet has come to represent

---

[29] Kleiner, *The Undivine Comedy*; Wiktor Weintraub, "Krasiński and Reeve," *The Polish Review*, V, No. 2 (Spring, 1960).

the most meaningful form of existence. In a society increasingly shorn of values poetic creation becomes the main repository of value, a spiritual oasis, the last refuge for men of imagination and sensibility. Thus in Romantic parlance poetry tends to serve as a metaphor for a stance, a way of life, an inherent human quality, rather than as a designation of a distinctive mode of endeavor, let alone a professional activity.

There is a some dialectical irony in this situation. First the poem, the creator's chief title to glory and indeed his only distinctive act, is hailed as a vessel of higher truth. Then the ultimate import of the poem is insisted upon so frenziedly and single-mindedly that the vessel itself eventually dwindles to the status of a mere plaything, an artifice or empty display. The Word overshadows words, the poet's proper medium and unique area of strength. The spirit of poetry is exalted at the expense of the letter.

This generalized, disembodied notion of poetry looms large in *The Undivine Comedy.* The narcissistic artist is arraigned on two counts which are disparate if not incompatible: he is taken to task both for subordinating life to art by applying to the former the misplaced aesthetic criterion of glamour, and for "making" poetry rather than living it. The true creator, we will recall, is the one in whom poetry dwells "unseen, unheard," who does not "separate himself from thy [poetry's] love by an abyss of words," while the false poet "delivers it [poetry] to the empty delight of men." Poetry, Krasiński seems to be suggesting, is an essence, a value to be attested to in daily living, to be internalized, as a modern psychologist would put it, rather than a vision to be embodied, a gift to be realized in a sensuous medium.

The distinction between the poet as a virtuoso and the poet as a witness or hero is stated in still more explicit and somewhat more pedestrian terms in Krasiński's little known short prose narrative, "Herburt" (1837), one of the author's few attempts at humor and social satire. There are two types of poets, muses Krasiński in a lengthy discursive passage, the morally warped and estranged virtuosi and the warm-hearted "poets of life," too full-blooded to abide by the frigid rigors of art. The former "will be hailed as craftsmen, for a multicolored rainbow plays upon the strings of their lyres which lacks but one string, that of the heart! What is such a bard amongst men? Perhaps a thunder, perhaps a rising sun or a heavenly dew, but never a brother amongst brothers!" The latter "take the entire world into their strong embrace. But art, patient like an old man, cold like an egotist, hard like a sculptor's chisel, withholds from them treasures gathered by dint of sly labors." [30]

"Poetry of action," a life worthy of the poet is morally superior to mere creativity: "I love Romeo but I would not shake hands with Shakespeare." [One wonders whether this astonishing statement was not due in part to aristocratic snobbery. Romeo's social status is better certified and probably more elevated than Shakespeare's.] "We may dislike Don Juan, but to Greece, to Greece we must sail with Byron!" [31]

Let us note further the curious semantics of a much-quoted passage from Krasiński's correspondence with H. Reeve. The document is doubly revealing since it exhibits both the self-conscious narcissistic glorying in the "poeticalness" of one's predicament—a habit which Krasiński scorns in his alter ego Count Henry—and the transpoetic stance toward which *The Undivine Comedy* is reaching. In a letter to Reeve, dated January, 1833, Krasiński declares:

Formerly we wished to become poetic creatures, today we must be moral beings, we must confront reality at all times and prepare for a struggle . . . between our thoughts and our actions. There is in this profound poetry. In this resignation, this pride, full of love, which is free from the bitter contempt shown mankind by some men of genius, I see boundless poetry and reach toward it with all

---

[30] *Dzieła Zygmunta Krasińskiego* [*Works of Z. Krasiński*], I, *Dzieła poetyckie* [*Poetry*] (Warszawa, 1934), 305.
[31] *Ibid.*, p. 306.

my heart. As for me, I will be a poet all my life, be I a farmer or a monk, rich or poor, a soldier or an officer. I was born a poet and I don't care if I will be appreciated or understood by anyone but you.[32]

Poetry has clearly become here a peculiarly dematerialized and deprofessionalized entity, independent of an actual creative achievement, of a poetic vocation or a literary public. If the chief protagonist of *The Undivine Comedy* turns each experience into a "song," his creator in his later and feebler works develops the habit of turning such words as "song" or "masterpiece" into honorific metaphors for lofty, meritorious, spiritually beautiful "experiences." In "The Unfinished Poem," a fragment from a projected trilogy of which *The Undivine Comedy* was to constitute the middle part, the "young man," a more redeemable version of Count Henry, is apostrophied thus by his older friend and mentor: "Henry! think what a joy it is to be able to exclaim in beholding a soul: 'Thou art beautiful! Give such a happiness to thy brothers! Be amongst them a masterpiece.'"[33] The notion of life as a masterpiece is an important motif in "The Dawn" (1843), the credo of the late Krasiński, half love-poem, half mystical vision of Poland's impending resurrection: "Yet the word is but a meager portion of life's masterpieces."[34] Later, in the epilogue to the poem, Krasiński intones, turning toward his "Beatrice," Delfina Potocka: "But thou, oh beauty, that I loved so well, / The only sister of my life, / Watch over me, be with me until I / Perish a fragment in the masterpiece of toils, / Die a stanza in the hymn of sacrifice."[35] Once again

---

[32] Krasiński et Reeve, *Correspondence*, II, 32–33.
[33] *Wiek XIX—Sto Lat Myśli Polskiej* (Warszawa, 1901), V, 387.
[34] *Dzieła Zygmunta Krasińskiego*, I, 354.
[35]   Lecz ty, piękności, którą ukochałem,
      Siostro jedyna w mojem życiu całem,
      .   .   .   .

      Czuwaj nademną—i zostań się przy mnie,
      Aż zginę cząstką w trudów arcydziele—
      Aż skonam zwrotką w poświęcenia hymnie!

                                        (*Ibid.*, p. 355.)

literary terminology ("masterpiece," "stanza," "hymn")
serves here to project the image of a higher spiritual attainment, of a good, "beautiful" life. No wonder the note on
which the poem ends is farewell to poetry in the strict sense of
the word: "Now other worlds lie open before us. / Perish my
songs, rise my deeds!"[36]

To a Polish literary historian Krasiński's obsessive emphasis
on the *acta-non-verba* theme, characteristically incongruous as
it is with the poet's ineffectuality which at times seemed to
verge on a paralysis of will, has special implications. A Krasiński scholar will point out, without necessarily using the term,
the compensatory nature of this harping on action, by invoking
the gnawing sense of guilt over the enforced aloofness from
the Polish uprising of 1830–31, the climactic deed of the Romantic generation, and the burning shame over his Father's
collaboration with the enemy. (When in November, 1830, the
Warsaw patriots rose against the Tsar, Wincenty Krasiński,
whether out of principled conformism or craven opportunism,
prevailed upon his son to refrain from participation in the
fighting. After a protracted conflict Zygmunt bowed to the
General's will, but the wound never healed. The disagreement
caused the first major crisis in the intimate and difficult relationship between the affectionate, but domineering, father and
the weak, hypersensitive son.) A student of Polish Romanticism will look beyond Krasiński's personal predicament toward the larger dilemma of the early nineteenth-century Polish
bard, an especially dramatic and acute example of the glories
and pitfalls of "engagement." He will point to another paradoxical situation. It is as an artist, as a wielder of memorable
speech, that the Polish Romantic poet rose to the position of
spiritual leadership of an embattled people, to claim with Adam
Mickiewicz's Konrad ("The Forefathers Eve") the "mastery
of souls." Yet the very urgency of his patriotic commitment,

[36] *Ibid.*

his very success in projecting the image of action, of struggle
against the enemy, as the only way of life worthy of a man
and a Pole made mere poetry appear frivolous, indeed irrelevant. Poetry was superseding itself, calling for its own liquida-
tion, overwhelmed by the burden of its own message. Hence
the strange case of Adam Mickiewicz, Poland's greatest poet,
who in his late thirties, after having produced his epic masterpiece "*Pan Tadeusz*," virtually stopped writing poetry to de-
vote himself during the remaining twenty years of his life to
journalism, teaching, religious reform, and frantic attempts at
direct action. Careful scholars such as W. Weintraub may still
wonder if Mickiewicz's prolonged silence was primarily a matter
of deliberate renunciation or of a gradual erosion of the poet's
creative powers.[37] Yet the myth of Mickiewicz the prophet
celebrates a national bard who gave up "words" for the sake
of "deeds." As is often the case, the legend has some basis
in reality: Did not Mickiewicz write in 1835 shortly before
giving up poetry, "the time will come when it will be necessary
to become a saint in order to be a poet?"[38]

A poet as an apprentice saint looking hopefully toward an
era where saints would be apprentice poets, here was a syndrome typical of post-1830 Polish Romantic poetry, with its
mixture of fervent if often heterodox Christian faith and glow-
ing patriotic dedication. In Mickiewicz, in the late Krasiński,
and in Słowacki, action means political or military struggle for
freedom or else individual sacrifice, renunciation, purification.
For an English Romantic it is more often than not a matter
of self-realization, "soul-making" (Keats) or untrammelled
self-expression, an outrageously exhibitionistic display of genuine or imaginary passions (Byron). "I verily believe," says
Byron in a letter to a friend, "that not you or any man of
poetical temperament can avoid a strong passion of some kind.

[37] Wiktor Weintraub, *The Poetry of Adam Mickiewicz* (The Hague, 1955), pp. 280–81.
[38] *Ibid.*, p. 280.

It is the poetry of life." [39] Elsewhere he expresses his preference
for active life in accents in which the Romantic cult of experience blends with the British gentleman's snobbish disdain for
mere " scribblers ": " Actions, actions, actions, I say, and not
writing, least of all rhyme. Look at the querulous and monotonous lives of the genus, except Cervantes, Tasso, Dante,
Ariosto, Kleist, Aeschylos, Sophocles, what a worthless, idle
brood it is! " [40]

The target and scope of action postulated or longed for
varied, depending on historical circumstances, on the cultural
pattern or the poet's personal predicament. Yet be he Krasiński or Byron, Mickiewicz or Keats, the worship of the creator
mediated through the infatuation with the " poetry of life "
tended to usher in the myth of the life of the poet. The spectacle which enacts this myth—now a secular pageant, now a
morality play—serves as dramatic testimony to the truth which
the outside world allegedly is busy suppressing, denying or
ignoring.

4.

The urge to blur the boundary between art and life and the
sense of moral alienation from the " breathing flesh " (*Manfred*), though characteristically Romantic phenomena, outlived
the Romantic movement. Thus Krasiński's anguished memento
points past the well-modulated despair of that accomplished
renegade Romantic Gustave Flaubert ("The artist is a mon-
strosity standing outside nature! "), toward the actual predicament and the self-conscious mythology of the twentieth-century
writer.

Since relevant examples are many, our associations are
bound to be arbitrary. In his already cited essay [41] Professor

[39] *Byronic Thoughts*, ed. P. Quennell (New York, 1960), p. 41. [My italics.]
[40] *Ibid.*, p. 35.
[41] " Stulecie ' Nieboskiej Komedji ' " [see fn. 2].

Górski draws a parallel between Krasiński's concept of the poet and Mauriac's complaint about the threat which the novelist's craft presents to the integrity of the writer's personality (" He enacts all his characters, transforming himself now into a demon, now into an angel. . . . Ultimately he cannot be anyone or anything, since he can be everything ").[42] The analogy is obvious: Mauriac, too, is concerned about the human price exacted by the literary vocation. Yet the French novelist's terms of reference, his emphasis on the protean nature of the man of letters are reminiscent of Keats rather than of Krasiński. To my mind, Krasiński's concern with the practicing poet's emotional aridity finds a closer counterpart in the work of another master of the twentieth-century novel, a writer who throughout his entire career was preoccupied with the problem of the artist in the bourgeois world. I am speaking, of course, of Thomas Mann.

The notion of art as a destructive force appears in all the major works of Mann, from *Buddenbrooks* down to *Dr. Faustus*. Commitment to writing is viewed here as a double threat: the artist's inevitable fascination with the Dionysian, the morbid and the irrational, saps the will, debilitates energy and undermines ego controls. At the same time, aesthetic detachment, the urge to express or articulate experience militates against emotional spontaneity.

The most significant statement of this latter danger is found in Mann's early tale " Tonio Kröger," a story of a sensitive young writer who, not unlike the author, is born into the family of a Lübeck grain merchant only to be " chosen against his will by the spirit of art " (E. Heller)[43] and thus estranged, if not altogether divorced, from his solid burgher background. His malaise, his deep-seated resentment of the crippling rigors imposed upon him by the literary craft, explode in a climactic

[42] François Mauriac, " Le Romancier et ses personnages," *Oeuvres complètes* (Paris, 1950), VIII, 287–328.
[43] Erich Heller, *The Ironic German* (London, 1958).

scene where Tonio lays his soul bare to a Russian woman painter, Lizaveta Ivanovna. (The choice of the audience seems revealing: the "Russian" may well stand in this context for Bohemian "madness," for an unambiguous and insouciant rejection of Western middle-class respectability):

Don't talk about "calling," Lizaveta Ivanovna. Literature is not a calling, it is a curse believe me![44] [It is a curse] because the artist must be inhuman, extrahuman. The very gift of style, formal expression is nothing else than a cool and fastidious attitude toward humanity; you might say there is this impoverishment and heredity as a preliminary condition. It is all up with the artist as soon as he becomes a man and begins to feel. I tell you, I am often sick to death of depicting humanity without having any part or lot in it. [Then comes the final blow:] To see things clearly, if even through your tears, to recognize, notice, observe and have to put it all down in a smile, at the very moment when hands are clinging and lips meeting and the human gaze is blinded with feeling—it is infamous, Lizaveta, it is indecent, outrageous![45]

Once again the tragic flaw of a "foreordained and doomed" artist is the loss of spontaneity, inability to register a direct emotional response.

To be sure, Tonio Kröger is a post-Romantic figure, a bourgeois artist. Not only is he less flamboyant or Byronically somber, and less given to self-dramatization, than is Krasiński's hero (Tonio's sin is not "acting a part," but spectatorship). He has, moreover, a better insight into his own predicament than Count Henry was ever capable of achieving, since he has the benefit of Thomas Mann's moral awareness. (In *The Undivine Comedy* it is the author and "voices from beyond" rather than the protagonist himself who articulate the judgment.) Nor does Mann's hero share Count Henry's aristocratic contempt for the common herd. In fact, Tonio's trouble is not heartlessness or *hubris*—that is why in spite of his protes-

---

[44] Thomas Mann, *Death in Venice and Seven Other Stories* (New York, 1960), p. 99.
[45] *Ibid.*, pp. 98, 102.

tations of doom he is probably redeemable—but unrequited love. For this escapee from Lübeck *bourgeoisie* is hopelessly and nostalgically in love with the world he left behind, with innocence, wholeness, and spontaneity, qualities which he attributes righly or wrongly to the unreflective and simple-minded, his handsome and athletic schoolmate Hans Hansen and the fair-haired Ingeborg Holm. Yet Ingeborg will respond promptly to Hans and turn away from Tonio's brooding gaze: in her world, the world of action and sensuous movement or, to be specific, on the dance floor, Tonio's awkward sophistication is no match for Hans's animal grace.

However essential the differences, the ultimate results are very similar indeed. In Mann's story and in Krasiński's drama alike, the artistic vocation and the price which it exacts proves a decisive barrier to normal human contact.

If Tonio Kröger's confession harks back to Count Henry's dilemma, the wan figure of Orcio, the doomed child-poet, finds a surprisingly close equivalent in that frail musical genius, the first in Mann's gallery of artists, Hanno Buddenbrook. Both Orcio and Hanno are last links in broken chains of generations, last heirs to decaying family traditions. Both die early; Hanno pays the price of a rapidly consuming typhoid fever for a moment of strenuous abandon to Wagner's Dionysian frenzy; Orcio is struck by the enemy's stray bullet, an innocent victim of his father's splendid yet ruthless determination. In either case the premature death is symbolic of the curse which hangs over the children-artists. They were not meant for this world; they were too frail, too vulnerable, too helpless to be able to survive amidst the bloody turmoil of social strife or in the rough-and-tumble world of business competition. Each during the short span of time allotted to him lives in a world of his own, seeking refuge from sordid material reality in his inner life, be it the universe of music (Hanno) or the realm of dreams and prophecies (Orcio) .

In Krasiński's drama the symbolism is naturally starker:

blindness which befalls Orcio at the age of ten—though undoubtedly a magnified echo of Krasiński's own disabilities and fears—is used to underscore the child's complete isolation from the outside world, his being blind to material contingency, as J. Klaczko puts it in one of the first serious essays on Krasiński.[46] This ignorance of all things mundane is coupled with, if not compensated by, an inward gaze, an uncanny moral sensitivity, indeed clairvoyance. Orcio is literally out of touch with his peers and with the world of the senses, but he has an "inside track" on the supernatural, he is in communication with the world of spirits. As Lednicki reminded us recently, "in the scene where Count Henry is with his son Orcio, with whom he is descending into the underground of the castle, the poet causes the vision of the last judgment [his father's trial] to appear before Orcio's prophetic eyes."[47]

The Gothic horrors of Krasiński's drama have no direct counterpart in Mann's bourgeois novel. Yet here, too, the alienated child-artist combines utter helplessness in everyday matters with remarkable moral perspicacity. He may not commune with the spirits, but he has an uncomfortable capacity to see beneath the surface. There is a telling scene in the novel where Hanno's capable and resourceful father Thomas Buddenbrook takes the boy along on a string of perfunctory but "useful" social calls. Hanno is expected to note and admire the social ease, urbanity and self-assurance of an accomplished man of affairs. Yet inwardly, little Hanno refuses to play the game. He cannot help but sense beneath the apparently effortless performance the strain and the weariness of a profoundly dispirited man.

Is moral sensitivity thus a reward for physical frailty and disease? Or, conversely, is the latter a penalty for having peered into the forbidden realm? Krasiński seems to have

---

[46] "La poésie polonaise du 19ème siècle et le poète anonyme," *Revue des deux Mondes*, XXXVII (1862), 23.
[47] Lednicki, "The Undivine Comedy," p. 131.

thought so. "One pays a heavy price for getting mixed up in the success of the gods," he wrote to Henry Reeve on April 4, 1833.[48]

5.

Toward the end of the memorable conversation between Tonio Kröger and Lizaveta Ivanova, the Russian briefly comes into her own. She listened with a rather unRussian restraint to Tonio's long jeremiad. Now it is her turn to diagnose her friend's "problem." "The solution," she says, "is that you are simply a bourgeois on the wrong path, a *bourgeois manqué*."[49]

This striking phrase, though clearly a polemical Bohemian simplification, seems to contain an important grain of truth, as Tonio will soon admit, indeed affirm, with a peculiar mixture of embarrassment and pride, in a letter to Lizaveta, which concludes the story. Having taken another plunge into the world of Hans and Ingeborg only to emerge once more a wistful outsider, Tonio seeks to come to terms with his "profoundly ambiguous" predicament. He describes himself as a "bourgeois who strayed off into art, a Bohemian who feels nostalgic yearnings for respectability, an artist with a bad conscience." "For surely it is my bourgeois conscience which makes me see in the artist's life, in all irregularity and all genius, something profoundly suspect, profoundly disreputable, that fills me with this lovelorn *faiblesse* for the simple and good, comfortable and normal, the average unendowed respectable human being." Curiously enough, the story ends on a vaguely positive note: "for if anything is capable of making a poet out of a *littérateur* it is my burgher's love of the human, the living and the usual."[50]

[48] Krasiński et Reeve, *Correspondance*, II, 64.
[49] Mann, *Death in Venice*, p. 106.
[50] *Ibid.*, p. 133.

Thus speaks Tonio Kröger. As Erich Heller shrewdly suggests, Mann's or Kröger's tendency to oversentimentalize the concept of the burgher may have led to a slight misstatement of the problem.[51] Tonio's unrequited love for the blond and the blue-eyed Ingeborg is the poet's rather than the burgher's. Poets, it seems, are more given to nostalgia than are burghers; they are also more likely to long for what they are not, and to imagine themselves in love with it. Yet Mann's half-serious, half-ironical eulogy of dual allegiance or, if one will, of subcultural ambivalence does give one a pause.

Have we not strayed, however, a bit too far from our principal subject? Does the spectacle of Tonio Kröger or Thomas Mann, for that matter, shuttling uneasily between the bourgeois and the Bohemian, bear any significant relation to the predicament and the self-image of the Polish aristocratic poet? I believe it does.

The differences between the two situations in terms of historical and social *realia* are too obvious to be insisted upon. The Buddenbrook ethos would have held little attraction for Zygmunt Krasiński. Both as a nostalgic Romanticist and as a scion of an old aristocratic family, he abhorred anything that smacked of commercialism. His letters are full of railing about the imminent ascendancy of merchants and bankers,[52] which becomes one of the major themes in his standing quarrel with the nineteenth century. Clearly the *tertium comparationis* here is not the nature of the formative environment, but the degree of its emotional hold on the poet and its attitude toward the life of imagination. There may well be some basis for analogy here. For it seems that Krasiński, not unlike Mann, was morally caught halfway between the world of his ancestors and that of poetry; that he, too, in Heller's words, had "roots in the social order at odds with the free play of imagination."[53]

---

[51] Heller, *The Ironic German*, pp. 74–75.

[52] " Ce siècle est le siècle des oppresseurs et des banquiers " (Krasiński et Reeve, *Correspondance*, I, 188).

[53] *The Ironic German*, p. 33.

In this latter respect the cleavage between a glittering Polish general and a late-nineteenth-century prosperous German merchant was none too essential. By the end of the century the Lübeck upper middle class was sufficiently entrenched and secure to be able to appreciate the finer things in life, including the arts. Yet even to the relatively urbane Hanseatic man of affairs, art was a status symbol or a luxury to be patronized or even indulged in occasionally, but scarcely a "sensible" full-time occupation. The attitude of Krasiński's father was not too dissimilar. In the salon which the suave soldier-diplomat maintained in Warsaw in the 1820's on the eve of a decisive break with the Polish public opinion, he liked to play the part of a patron of the arts, to surround himself with men of letters, be it of pseudo-classicist or early Romantic persuasion. Yet, he too seems to have regarded poetry as an adornment rather than a serious pursuit worthy of a grown man's, let alone a Krasiński's, best energies. The poet's sober friend Danielewicz must have been addressing himself or catering to some such attitude in the General when in a detailed report on Zygmunt's typical day he was assuring him: "we do not talk about poetry or romance, but about serious matters."[54] We will recall that the same Danielewicz in another letter to Wincenty Krasiński expressed satisfaction over Zygmunt's alleged intention to present the poet in a somewhat preposterous light.[55] The attitude which underlies such *dicta* appears to be one of a tough-minded gentleman to whom a professional poet is something of a "sissy."

Most biographical accounts produce the impression that, however deviant Krasiński's inner life and occasionally his outward behavior may have been, and however remarkable his speculative intelligence, he never managed to shake himself loose from the impact of his father's value-pattern, to shed the fascination with the model presented by Wincenty Krasiński. An aristocrat who gloried in the real or imaginary past of his

---

[54] Quoted in Kallenbach, *Z. Krasiński.*   [55] *Ibid.*

class but was, especially in *The Undivine Comedy*, harshly
critical of its present, who worshipped poetry but never became
part of the literary milieu, Krasiński could echo or rather anticipate Tonio Kröger's complaint: "I stand between two worlds.
I am at home in neither."[56]

To pursue the analogy, if Tonio Kröger is a bourgeois
manqué, Krasiński was in a sense a frustrated soldier as well
as a frustrated saint. In fact, it could be argued that when
in *The Undivine Comedy* he questions the human dignity of
the poet's calling, he does so both from "above" and from
"below." When he discourages "words, words, words" in
behalf of action, he is motivated primarily by a lofty idea of
poetry which I was trying to outline above. But he may not
be altogether unmindful of the aristocratic military code which
sees in deeds of valor the only ultimate test of man's real worth.
Krasiński's biographers tell us about the frail young poet's early
dreams of glory, his hankering for military exploits.[57] "I weep
for fame," avers one of his mouthpieces in an early, immature
work, "Wladyslaw Herman and His Court." Since physical
disability, coupled with paternal fiats, barred him from the
battlefield—the only arena in which he could emulate his
father, earn his respect, and at the same time effectively challenge his authority—poetic fame must have often appeared to
the ambitious youth as a mere substitute, a second choice.

Was the conflict of values which may have been engendered
thus an element of weakness or an additional source of strength
as Tonio Kröger thought his ambivalence to be? Or, more
broadly, can dual allegiance—hovering between two worlds—
ever be a boon for a man of letters? Does not partial dependence upon a social code distrustful of the creative imagination
court the danger of excessive susceptibility to hostile stereo-
types of the artist, of self-hatred or, at the very least, confusion
as to one's identity and primary allegiance?

---

[56] Mann, *Death in Venice*, p. 133.
[57] See especially, B. Chlebowski, "Z. Krasiński," *Sto Lat Mysli Polskiej*, V
(Warszawa, 1909).

The implications of these queries are too vast to be confronted here. All I can say at this point is that ambivalence, that is, a conflict of values, need not be equated with a confusion of values. The latter is always a handicap as it leads inevitabliy to a blurring of the writer's moral vision. The former, if illuminated by insight and held in check by an overriding commitment to the creative life, can be an asset for the writer to the extent that it contributes to a more flexible, comprehensive or dialectical view of reality. Thomas Mann's massive achievement argues strongly for this possibility. Tonio Kröger was not altogether wrong. For one cannot help but speculate as to the extent to which Mann's residual affinity for the world of the Buddenbrooks and his concomitant unwillingness to identify himself unequivocally with the Bohemian garret accounts for the richly rewarding ironies and ambiguities in his treatment of the modern artist's dilemma.

For Krasiński the shuttling between two disparate social codes was only one of the many inner conflicts. Indeed the career of this high-strung, introspective bard, who reached his peak at the age of twenty-one only to decline gradually into the insipid versifying and abstract rhetoric of "The Dawn" and "The Psalms of the Future," is a tangle of contradictions, a web of paradoxes. A frail, hypochondriac, indecisive young man daydreaming about military fame ("I was born for glory"); a poet consumed by overweening hunger for recognition and acclaim and yet compelled to publish his works anonymously or under assumed names so as not to jeopardize General Krasiński's standing and not to be handicapped by his reputation; a patriot caught between a passionate urge to serve his country and "follow Christ" and loyalty toward an affectionate but tyrannical father; a moralist reaching forever toward Christian love and charity, but full of resentment and self-pity, he is one of the most anguished, neurotic personalities in the Romantic movement.

Over the years the unresolved conflicts must have taken a

heavy toll, sapping as they did the poet's vital energy, impeding the free play of his imagination. At a late stage of his career he sees his " heart "—apparently his affection and compassion for his father who stood between the poet and the Polish public opinion—as the main source of his misery. "For I have a heart," he wailed in a letter to Delfina Potocka, "and it destroyed me. Here lies the clue to my lack of energy, to my perennial misery. Since I cannot get drunk [anymore] on concepts, ideas, sounds!" [58] Another letter written at about the same time laments the wasted potentialities. "Weep over me, for I could have been a monument, . . . but all there is now is rubble, pain and inner split, and soon there will be nothing at all." [59]

Even if due allowance is made for the possible effects of momentary depression, melodramatic exaggeration, and self-pity, the gradual deterioration of Krasiński's artistry since the late thirties is an incontrovertible fact. This erosion of creative powers is amply attested to in the increasing vagueness of imagery and rhythmical monotomy of Krasiński's later verse and last but not least in his pathetic attempts to recapture his finest hour by reviving *The Undivine Comedy* themes within a broadly conceived dramatic trilogy which, needless to say, never materialized.

Has the poet's initial *élan* disintegrated under the cumulative impact of external pressures and inner tensions? A provocative recent essay offers a somewhat different solution to the Krasiński riddle. In "Krasiński's Retreat" [60] a contemporary Polish poet and critic Czeslaw Miłosz argues persuasively that *The Undivine Comedy* is Krasiński's only work in which he dared to confront his "fear neurosis," to look into his personal hell. Having done so, continues Miłosz, he recoiled in panic only to spend the rest of his life seeking refuge from the pro-

---

[58] Quoted in, *Dziela Z. Krasińskiego*, I, vii.
[59] *Ibid.*
[60] *The Polish Review*, 1959 [see fn. 1].

foundly disturbing insight and, more broadly, from the world of senses, in vaporous philosophizing and vague, mystical visions.

Once again, it seems, ambivalence clarified by awareness proves fertile; confusion, or worse still, self-deception, debilitating. For if Miłosz is right, it was the ability of the young man who wrote *The Undivine Comedy* to face his predicament that enabled him to control his conflicts and transmute them into art.

Be that as it may, the salient fact remains that several years before the decline seems to have set in, in the wake of a major crisis in his life which brought him face to face with the true nature of paternal authority, Krasiński found himself for the first and last time in a position to utilize creatively his frustrations and anxieties rather than be victimized or crushed by them. Out of his growing fear of the "people"—the sullen masses which loomed on the horizon as an ominous threat to the world he was born into—he created a powerful social drama which in the unrelieved starkness of its moral alternatives often reaches the proportions of tragedy. Out of a vague sense of guilt over his own Romantic posturing and a deep-seated ambivalence toward his role and responsibility as an artist, he fashioned, in a momentary blaze of painful insight, one of the most compelling statements of the poet's moral dilemma to be found in the nineteenth-century literature.

4. THE MAKER AND THE SEER:

TWO RUSSIAN SYMBOLISTS

" Le monde doit aboutir à un livre." (Mallarmé)
*" The fallen angel-demon was the world's
first lyrist."* (Blok, " On Lyric Poetry ")

1.

In his retrospective essay "L'Existence du Symbolisme,"[1]
Valéry described symbolism as a conglomeration of disparate
styles and creative personalities rather than a coherent aesthetic entity. The Symbolist movement, argued Valéry, was
both more and less than a literary school. Separated by their
aesthetics, the Symbolists were held together by their ethics,
that is, by a " common rejection of an appeal to majority," of
commercial, Philistine values.

Though it would be unwise to ignore so authoritative a testimony, it need not be accepted without reservations. The Symbolist poets were substantially closer to each other in their
stylistic devices, indeed in their underlying attitude toward
poetic language, than Valéry's *dicta* seem to suggest. Suffice
it to mention the Symbolist's tendency to treat the metaphor
as a vehicle of esoteric correspondences, to evoke rather than
to name, to suggest rather than to describe; in a word, to use
verbal "music," the fluid auditory and visual imagery, so as

[1] Paul Valéry (1938), *Oeuvres* (Paris, 1957), I, 686–706.

to enhance the emotional suggestiveness and the associative wealth of the poetic idiom.

And yet in one sense Valéry was more right than wrong. Symbolism was as much a stance as it was a style. By the end of the century the cleavage between the artist and his society—which had set in during the Romantic age—seems complete and irrevocable. Under the aegis of the new sensibility the estrangement from the bourgeois becomes the poet's essential characteristic, a badge of distinction, an article of faith.

From France came the most influential variants of the modern myth of the embattled artist—the images of the poet as an ivory-tower hermit (Mallarmé), an outcast (Verlaine), a rebel and a seer (Rimbaud). But the ethical aspect of symbolism found its most poignant expression in the poetry of the Russian "Silver age" (1895–1914).

A student of this fascinating period has at his disposal a remarkable wealth of vivid and suggestive eyewitness testimony supplied by brilliant, if not always reliable, protagonists such as Andrei Belyi,[2] philosophical fellow travelers of symbolism, e. g., Fëdor Stepun[3] and post-Symbolist poet-critics (Khodasevich, Tsvetaeva).[4] Though some of these recollections are marred by special pleading and colored by a strong personal bias, they add up to what is probably the most distinguished body of memoir literature to be brought to bear upon a single period of Russian intellectual history.

One of the salient characteristics of the Symbolist era as recorded by these perceptive observers is the pervasive urge to

[2] Andrei Belyi, *Na rubezhe dvukh stoletii* [*At the Crossroads of Two Centuries*] (Moscow-Leningrad, 1920); *Nachalo veka* [*The Beginning of a Century*] (Moscow, 1933); *Mezhdu dvukh revoliutsii* [*Between Two Revolutions*] (Leningrad, 1934).

[3] Fëdor Stepun, *Byvshee i nesbyvsheesia* [*My Life: Realities and Dreams*] (New York, 1956).

[4] Vladislav Khodasevich, *Nekropol'* (Bruxelles, 1939); *Literaturnye stat'i i vospominaniia* [*Literary Articles and Reminiscences*] (New York, 1954); Marina Tsvetaeva, *Proza* [*Prose*] (New York, 1953).

blur the boundary between life and art. "Symbolism," says Khodasevich, in his *Literaturnye stat'i i vospominaniia*,[5] "cannot be fully reconstructed, indeed comprehended as a purely literary phenomenon." Elsewhere he developed this notion more fully: "Symbolism did not want to separate the writer from the man, a literary biography from a personal one. Symbolism was not content to be a school of poetry, a literary movement; it sought to become a mode of creating life, and in this lay its deepest and most elusive truth . . ."[6] "[symbolism] stubbornly sought in its milieu a genius who would manage to fuse life and art. We know now that such a genius was never found, that the formula was never discovered."[7] During the decadent era," chimes in Fëdor Stepun, "people, especially women, did not believe that there should be any discrepancy between words and deeds." According to Stepun, this tendency to equate or confuse two levels of reality entailed considerable peril. Insistence that a real-life romance develop with the relentless consistency of a literary plot had obvious pitfalls. The price of "transforming an aesthetic canon into a moral code" was often extravagantly high.[8]

In the feverishly intense atmosphere of prewar literary Petersburg or Moscow, *Dichtung* and *Wahrheit* were precariously intertwined, with the poet's biography turning now into a Passion play, now into the testing ground for the poem.

The availability of these two solutions to the turn-of-the-century art vs. life dilemma reflects the existence of what Viacheslav Ivanov called "two strands in Russian Symbolism."[9] This duality has often been discussed in chronological terms as a cleavage between the older Symbolists (Briusov, Balmont) and the younger ones (Blok, Belyi), or else

[5] Khodasevich, *Literary Articles* . . . , p. 15.

[6] Khodasevich, *Nekropol'*, p. 8.

[7] *Ibid.*

[8] Stepun, *Byvshee i nesbyvsheesia*, p. 319.

[9] "Dve stikhii v russkom simvolizme," *Po zvezdam [By the Stars]* (St. Petersburg, 1909), pp. 247–308.

between decadents and Symbolists proper. Whatever the labels, substantively the dichotomy has been diagnosed as one of French-oriented aestheticism vs. a thrust toward a supra-aesthetic metaphysics.[10] The two variants of the Russian Symbolist mentality clashed openly in 1910, on the pages of the Modernist journal *Apollon*. Speaking for the metaphysicians, the hieratic poet-scholar V. Ivanov insisted that "Symbolism did not want to be and could not be merely art."[11] The *maître* of Moscow Symbolists, the tireless, versatile, resourceful Valerii Briusov emphatically disagreed: "Symbolism wanted to be and was only art. Art is autonomous; it has its own methods and its own tasks."[12]

Thus the issue was joined. For the older Symbolist art was the supreme, indeed the only, viable value, if not a substitute religion. To an Ivanov, a Belyi, a Blok poetry appeared as a singularly appropriate vehicle of a transpoetic revelation, of a heterodox mystique. By the same token, if the aesthete believed with Mallarmé that the world could be vindicated or given meaning only by "adding up to a Book" ("*le monde doit aboutir à un livre*"), their opponents saw in the life of the poet an enactment of, or a living testimony to, that "transformation of the world"[13] which a truly poetic vision seeks to embody or prefigure.

The former stance, which I would like to call Parnassian, found its most influential and articulate exponent in Valerii Briusov. The Dionysian conception of the poet is most poignantly exemplified by the career of Aleksandr Blok.

[10] Johannes Holthusen, *Studien zur Aesthetik und Poetik des russischen Symbolismus* (Goettingen, 1951); Georgette Donchin, *The Influence of French Symbolism on Russian Poetry* (The Hague, 1959); Renato Poggioli, *The Poets of Russia, 1890–1930* (Cambridge, Mass., 1960).

[11] "Zavety simvolizma" [The Tenets of Symbolism], *Apollon* (May–June, 1910), No. 8, pp. 5–20.

[12] "O rabskoi rechi. V zashchitu poèzii" [About the Slaves' Speech. In Defense of Poetry], *Apollon*, No. 9 (July–August, 1910), pp. 31–34.

[13] Quoted from, Johannes Holthusen, *Fëdor Sologub's Roman-Trilogie, " Tvorimaia Legenda"*: *aus der Geschichte des russischen Symbolismus* (The Hague, 1958).

2.

In 1907, at the height of his influence as literary pundit and pace-setter, Briusov produced his much quoted credo " To the Poet." Here is a rough English prose approximation of what the *maître* had to say to an imaginary apprentice:

You must be proud as a banner / You must be sharp as a sword / Like Dante's, your cheeks must / Be scorched by subterranean flame.

Be an impassive witness of all / Encompassing all in your gaze / Let your supreme virtue be / Your readiness to mount the stake.

Perhaps, everything in life is but a means / To brightly singing verses. And from your carefree childhood on / [You must] seek combinations of words.

At moments of love embraces / Force yourself to be dispassionate. And in the hours of ruthless crucifixions / Sing the glory of frenzied pain.

In morning dreams and in the evening abyss / Seize the whispers of fate. And remember: for ages has the Poet's sacred wreath been made of thorns.[14]

---

[14]   Ты должен быть гордым, как знамя;
        Ты должен быть острым, как меч;
        Как Данту, подземное пламя
        Должно тебе щеки обжечь.

        Всего будь холодный свидетель,
        На все устремляя свой взор.
        Да будет твоя добродетель
        Готовность взойти на костер.

        Быть может, все в жизни лишь средство
        Для ярко певучих стихов,
        И ты с беспечального детства
        Ищи сочетания слов.

        В минуты любовных обьятий
        К бесстрастью себя приневоль,
        И в час беспощадных распятий
        Прославь исступленную боль.

Let us note, at the outset, that Briusov's *ars poetica* is concerned with the poet rather than with poetry. The central question here is not what kind of verse the devotee ought to write, but what kind of life he should lead, what manner of man he ought to be.

The two adjectives featured in the opening lines of the poem have a characteristically, if not uniquely, Briusovian ring. To be sure, the cluster of attitudes suggested by " proud "—pride in one's calling, spiritual intransigence and a sense of superiority vis-à-vis the *profanum vulgus*—can be traced back to Pushkin, indeed to Horace. Yet the combative assertiveness of the military similes (banner, sword) is clearly reminiscent of the man who thought of himself—and was widely thought of—as a standard-bearer of the Movement. Nor will " sharp," with its intimations of definiteness and incisiveness, come as a surprise to anyone familiar with the tenor of Briusov's work. Though on occasions he paid lip-service to the Symbolist cult of " nuance," his rhetorical and cerebral bent was fundamentally incompatible with the Verlainian vagueness and languor.

The subsequent two lines are a homage to the *Zeitgeist*. Whether or not the " subterranean flame " image is in fact, as Renato Poggioli surmises,[15] an echo of Baudelaire's " *paradis artificiels* " or Rimbaud's " *dérèglement des sens*," the phrase clearly points toward two interlocking turn-of-the-century themes—fascination with evil and the mystique of suffering. The latter emphasis is reinforced by " readiness to mount the stake " of the second stanza, the " ruthless crucifixions " in the fourth, and finally, the grim warning of the last quatrain.

В снах утра и в бездне вечерней
Лови, что шепнет тебе Рок,
И помни: от века из терний
Поэта заветный венок.

(Valerii Briusov, " Poètu " [To the Poet], *Izbrannye stikhotvoreniia* [*Selected Poems*] [Leningrad–Moscow, 1945], p. 173.)

[15] Poggioli, *Poets of Russia*, p. 102.

On the face of it, all this Christian symbolism seems to be oddly out of place in a poem whose key passage strongly suggests that "brightly singing verses" might be the only thing of value. Clearly, martyrdom as readiness to sacrifice oneself in behalf of what is generally recognized as a "cause," be it a religious or a secular one, is not at issue here. Are we thus justified in concluding that Briusov invokes the notion of sacrifice in vain? While the hyperbolical and hackneyed quality of Briusov's rhetoric is not to be gainsaid, such an inference might be a trifle premature.

Viewed at closer range, the semantics of "To the Poet" prove partly misleading. Briusov's argument does entail the motif of an ordeal, but characteristically, it is one which has less to do with the "hot" imagery (flame, stake) than with its opposite pole, notably the cluster revolving around the notion of coldness, detachment, noninvolvement.[16]

"Be an impassive witness of all / Encompassing all in your gaze," these lines highlight two crucial aspects of the stance which Briusov is urging upon the novice. The repetition of the inclusive pronoun "all" reflects an insistence on an indiscriminately comprehensive attitude toward life. The poet cannot afford to be choosy or squeamish, he must not shun any facet of human existence, however sordid, grim or repellent. (This, incidentally, might be the minimum interpretation of the Inferno image: "subterranean flame,"—pain, suffering, degradation, vice—is "part of the game.") The poet worthy of the name must be prepared to take in his stride, or expose himself to, all dimensions of reality.

Expose himself to reality, rather than fully experience it. The importance of this distinction scarcely needs to be elabo-

---

[16] The contrast between "coldness" and "heat," impassivity and frenzy, functions here as a compositional principle, with the first half of the stanza featuring the one motif and the second half the other. This thematic and rhetorical antinomy may be said to embody the notion of inclusiveness which is central to the poem: to encompass the entire range of experience is, in a sense, to shuttle between its opposite poles.

rated upon. Let us note that Briusov does not enjoin his imaginary disciple to plunge or leap into the flames. "Scorched cheeks" suggests surface contact, and properly so. For the poet is not expected here to be a full participant in the *agon*, but merely an "impassive witness." The code of behavior prescribed by Briusov rules out total emotional involvement.

The point is driven home with a somewhat chilling grimness in the fourth stanza: "At moments of love embraces force yourself to be dispassionate." Even in the most intimate experiences whose very integrity hinges on the participant's willingness and ability to let himself go, even in the moments of passion so assiduously celebrated by Briusov and his fellow Symbolists, the poet must not divest himself of his all-encompassing spectatorship. It is his duty—and his destiny—to withdraw a part of himself from the maelstrom of emotion in order to keep it cool, and thus available for observation, introspection, recording, mental note-taking. Otherwise, it seems, the encounter might go to waste, the love affair might fail to produce a love poem.

Experience is thus demoted to the status of mere raw material "for brightly singing verses," of a repertory of poetic themes. It becomes something to be manipulated, recorded, verbalized—in a word, used—rather than valued for its own sake. The Flaubert-Mallarmé life-for-art's-sake doctrine is proclaimed here with that relentless explicitness which is Briusov's trademark.

The keynote in this set of directives is self-discipline, a principle, we may add, which starts operating at a very early stage, as a matter of formative, existential choice. "And from your sorrow-free childhood on / [You must] seek combinations of words." For one who is not a poet, Briusov implies, childhood is indeed free of care and responsibility, a realm of unfocused, unpragmatic, disinterested play. But the child who is to be chosen cannot afford to play aimlessly, just for the fun of it. He must channel his natural proclivity for verbal play into a

search for the best words in the best order, so that in the ful-
ness of time they may glitter in his "brightly singing verses."

By now we may have a somewhat better idea as to the
kind of sacrifice which Briusov has in store for the poet. It is
a *sui generis* emotional asceticism, which plays havoc with
natural impulses. The poet is regarded here as a member of a
secular order. He is dedicated not to renunciation or withdrawal—since the life of the senses has to be fully explored
for the greater glory of poetry—but to a ruthless self-restraint.
What is surrendered here is emotional spontaneity, the right
available to normal people to give in to one's emotions, to
respond and experience freely, unencumbered by ulterior aesthetic designs, by the "stern commands of the Muse." In a
1911 poem "The Poet to the Muse" Briusov avers: "I have
betrayed much and many / I have abandoned banners in the
midst of a battle / But to your stern commands / My soul has
forever been faithful."[17]

To those who recall the plight of Krasiński's Count Henry
and Tonio Kröger's above quoted harangue[18] Briusov's ad-
monitions will have a familiar ring. Thomas Mann's story is
especially relevant here. Briusov's injunction "At moments
of love embraces force yourself to be dispassionate" urges an
attitude and describes a situation such as is decried by Tonio
Kröger in his famous outburst: "To see things clearly, if even
through your tears, to recognize, notice, observe and have to
put it all down with a smile at the very moment when hands
are clinging and lips meeting and the human gaze is blinded
with feeling. It is infamous, Lizaveta, it is indecent, outrageous!"[19]

[17]   Я изменял и многому и многим,
         Я покидал в час битвы знамена;
         Но день за днем твоим велениям строгим
         Душа была верна.

                    (Briusov, *Izbrannye stikhotvoreniia*, p. 245.)

[18] See above, pp. 57–58.

[19] *Death in Venice and Seven Other Stories* (New York, 1960).

It is hardly necessary to insist on the essential difference of underlying attitude between Krasiński and Mann on the one hand and Briusov on the other. All three are fundamentally at one in their assessment of the emotional cost of art. But what to Krasiński and Mann is a curse, a tragic flaw or an infamous moral failing, appears in "To the Poet" as a proudly won badge of distinction, a sign of aloofness from, and superiority to, the common herd. Let the self-indulgent Philistine, Briusov is saying in effect, indulge his emotions; he has nothing better to do. The "guardian of Mystery" must curb his common humanity in order to serve his demon the better. The credo culminates in a warning: Are you prepared to pay the price? Do you have the stamina which the poet's calling requires, the determination to subordinate your personal life to the stern demands of the Muse? If not, you need not apply.

3.

"Perhaps everything in life is but a means / To brightly singing verses. . . ." These lines were quoted *ad nauseam* in the pre-1914 Russian literary *cénacles*. In the atmosphere where the boundary between words and deeds, between love poems and love affairs was often blurred, the dictum of the Symbolist *maître* tended to acquire the authority of a guide to action. The notion that the poet has the right, indeed the duty, to use his life as material for his work, and to hoard momentary thrills in order to produce more and better love lyrics, was taken very seriously indeed by many adherents, and hangers-on of the movement, and last but not least by the master himself. The results—a freewheeling promiscuity and relative emotional shallowness of each "encounter"[20]—are easy to imagine.

[20] In a poem entitled "To Women," Briusov was declaiming thus: "Here are

Nor is it necessary to rely on conjectures. Shrewd, if not exactly sympathetic, eyewitnesses (e. g., Khodasevich and Tsvetaeva)—Briusov apparently was the kind of man that was more likely to evoke admiration or respect than affection— offer telling instances of Briusov's casual, not to say callous, attitude toward the targets of his wide-ranging sexual experimentation. On of the examples cited by Khodasevich [21] was the much-touted affair with a marginal poetess, Nadezhda Lvova, who apparently took the "encounter" much too seriously. Briusov's unruffled shuttling between domesticity and "the other woman" proved too much for the latter. Finally, the stealth and precariousness of the relationship drove her to suicide. Briusov promptly recovered from the shock only to embark upon another experience. In fact, as literary Moscow was buzzing with gossip about Lvova's suicide, Briusov was regaling the habitués at the Moscow Literary-Artistic Society with a rather cheery poem built around the proposition "Let the dead sleep peacefully in their coffins / While the living enjoy life. . . ." [22]

Moreover—and perhaps more important—Briusov's programmatic repudiation of a strong emotional involvement may well have contributed to the curious impersonality of his poetry. For all the richness of their orchestration, for all the polish and, occasionally, felicity with which the mature Briusov of *Urbi et Orbi* (1903) and *Stephanos* (1906) articulated the blatant, sultry, and morbid *fin-de-siècle* eroticism, these verses have a singularly hollow ring. Their sensuality is more convincing than their emotionality—apparently lust came more naturally to Briusov than love. But even passion, which is

you, sorrowful, proud shadows / Of Women deserted by me. / Oh! these arms and breasts and lips, / Curves of greedy bodies / I possessed you, I was your master! / ... In vain do you extend your hands toward me / You, doomed to eternal separation / I must live alone ..." (V. Briusov, *Puti i pereput'ia* [Moscow, 1908], pp. 40–41).

[21] Khodasevich, *Nekropol'*, pp. 45–48.

[22] Briusov, *Izbrannye stikhotvoreniia*, p. 49.

enshrined here as a supreme value in a world increasingly shorn of values,[23] is disconcertingly abstract and cliché-ridden. What we find in Briusov is not an imaginative recreation of the texture of " encounters " between two differentiated human beings, but a monotonous celebration of lust, now as an erotic witches' sabbath, now as a religious rite which offers a glimpse of mystery.

In his already quoted essay on Briusov [24] Khodasevich shows how the notion of love as a ritual leads inexorably to depersonalization. "We are high priests / We celebrate a rite" [lines from Briusov's much-quoted poem " The Road to Damascus "] —those are terrible words. For if what is involved is a rite, the identity of the partner does not matter. The "priestess of love " is Briusov's favorite expression. But the face of the priestess is covered. One priestess can be easily replaced by another; the rite will remain the same. Not being able to find a human being in these priestesses, Briusov cries, overcome by panic: " Trembling, I embrace a corpse. Love becomes torture. Where are we? / On a bed of passion or on a torture rack? " [25]

In many poems of Briusov sex is indeed an ordeal, a grim sacrificial duty performed with clenched teeth. Sacred terminology is invoked with monotonous obsession:

Let my lips cling to your humidly breathing lips / So that in silence could rise / My cherished temple.[26]

---

[23] A poem in *Stephanos, Venok [Stephanos, the Wreath]* (Moscow, 1906), contains the following eulogy of Mark Anthony: " Tribunes were vying for people's favor / and emperors for power / while you, beautiful, eternally young / erected but one altar, passion."

[24] Khodasevich, *Nekropol'*, pp. 26–60.

[25] Briusov, *Stephanos*, " In a Torture Chamber," p. 68.

[26]　Дай устам моим приникнуть
　К влажно дышащим устам,
　Чтоб в молчаньи мог возникнуть
　Мой заветный, тайный храм.

(Briusov, *Stephanos*, p. 87.)

To a heavenly Astarte, / Precursor of the morn . . . / I, a dark-eyed priest with a dark-curled sister, / Sing psalms day and night.[27]

The most genuine and unhackneyed aspect of these proceedings is the mounting despair, the frenzied clinging to the partner's body—a gesture which points up the lyrical hero's ultimate inability to break out of his isolation, to reach the "other."[28]

It would be grossly inaccurate to blame the tenor of these competent, but remarkably dated, exercises in eroticism on the doctrine proclaimed in "To the Poet." There is much in the above that is simply another tribute to the turn-of-the-century ethos, with its Baudelairian symbiosis of lust and pain, love and death, and the Symbolist conception of love as the ultimate experience, a short cut to the absolute. By the same token, the standard-bearer of the Symbolist movement could hardly be expected to have avoided one of the chief pitfalls of Symbolist rhetoric—the tendency to dissolve the tang of the actual into the haze of high-flown abstractions, of hieratic pontificating.

In a different vein, it could be argued that the ruthlessly instrumentalist message of Briusov's was simply a post-factum justification of his own temperamental proclivities. Most reliable observers seem to agree that in the man who wrote "To the Poet" sensual curiosity was much more in evidence than was either warmth or spontaneity.

Yet, on second thought, it might be wiser not to prejudge the nature of the causal connection between Briusov's alleged psychic make-up and his literary credo. Ideology, literary or

---

[27]   Астарте небесной, предвестнице утра,
Над нами сияющей ночью и днем,
Я—жрец темноглазый, с сестрой темнокудрой,
И ночью и днем воспеваю псалом.

(*Ibid.*, p. 84.)

[28] "Only one thing remains for us—to draw nigh / To blend our lips, to hang like grapes / To touch temples with a blasphemous hand / To weave one's body into Hephaestus' net." (Briusov, *Stephanos*, p. 83.)

otherwise, cannot be reduced with impunity to psychological or biographical considerations. Only two assertions can be made with relative certainty: a) Briusov's natural bent must have facilitated his espousal of the doctrine stated above; b) since ideas have consequences, especially for those who take them seriously, this commitment in turn was bound to accentuate the pre-existing behavior pattern by providing it with an ideological sanction, by making a poetic virtue out of a psychic necessity.

We are faced here, it seems, with a somewhat paradoxical situation. For to the extent that Briusov's single-minded dedication to "brightly singing verses" did affect his actual behavior, it tended to impoverish his emotional life by restricting further his congenitally limited ability and willingness to form deeper emotional relationships. By the same token, to the extent that the quality of Briusov's actual experiences can be assumed to have colored the texture of his love poems—and this is admittedly a moot point—Briusov's aestheticism may well have impaired the aesthetic worth of his erotic poetry. Let me make myself clear: what is at issue here is not the sincerity or truthfulness of a lyric, that is, its fidelity to a specific emotional actuality, but rather the poem's capacity to emulate the qualities inherent in any fully-textured emotional experience, to produce an illusion of individualized vibrancy, a sense of immediacy.

Was Briusov thus victimized by his adherence to the Parnassian doctrine? Not exactly. True, in his readiness to subordinate the natural claims of life to the stern exigencies of art as he interpreted them, Briusov was asserting the supreme importance of literary craft. Yet in Briusov and in many of his like-minded contemporaries the Flaubertian *impassibilité* was complicated if not distorted by implicit assumptions drawn from an entirely different intellectual and literary tradition.

The argument of "To the Poet" clearly presupposes the turn-of-the-century cult of experience—the belief that frenzied

accumulation of variegated thrills is tantamount to living a
full life, which in turn is incumbent upon the man of sensibility. Moreover, and, perhaps, more important, the notion
of hoarding experiences with a view to subsequent poetic expression is predicated upon an unexamined Romantic assump-
tion concerning the relationship between life and work. Only
one who views the lyric as fundamentally a transcript of an
actual emotional event can insist, as Briusov does in effect,
that an indiscriminately wide range of experience is a necessary
prerequisite for a variegated body of lyric verse. In fact, it
might be argued that the Romantic and neo-Romantic view
of the poetic process somewhere along the line tends to subvert
the Parnassian tenet about the essential autonomy of art.

The difference between Briusov's and Mallarmé's Flauber-
tianism thus becomes apparent. Mallarmé withdrew into the
ivory tower to keep his poetry pure and free from the vulgar
distractions and blandishments of the market place. Briusov
insisted on exposing himself, and his ideal poet, to any and all
emotional and sensory stimuli. A full and thrill-packed life
divested of spontaneity and of strong personal involvement is,
from the standpoint of the poet's basic humanity, a flawed,
indeed a self-contradictory affair. Was it also a self-defeating
one? One wonders. Ironically, it is precisely the assumptions
underlying Briusov's poetics that lend queries such as these
special relevance and authority.

4.

Yet to note the pitfalls and internal contradictions inherent
in Briusov's mythology of the poet is not necessarily to bemoan
the loss which may have resulted from his commitment to
"brightly singing verse." Judging by reliable testimony, on
balance Briusov had little to lose and a great deal to gain by

espousing a philosophy of life which set so much store by self-control. For Briusov was not merely a deliberate craftsman, a highly conscious " maker " rather than a " natural," seemingly effortless, singer of Balmont's variety, or a possessed seer such as Blok. He was, in the literal sense of the word, a self-made poet, not that he came from the ranks—Briusov's solid merchant background lacked the intellectual luster of Blok's family tradition, but it was not exactly underprivileged—but in that he made himself a distinguished man of letters, a poet, a novelist, a critic, a leader of an important school of poetry, as a matter of a deliberate choice, of an act of will, by dint of painstaking, unremitting toil. For it took nothing less than a dogged effort at mastering unfamiliar techniques, at attuning oneself to uncongenial attitudes, to turn this sober, incisive, unbending, fundamentally unlyrical and " unmusical " man into the captain of a literary movement which favored the ineffable, worshipped " music," and searched for a mystique. Sergei Gorodetskii, an erstwhile disciple turned heretic, called attention to this curious contrast between Briusov's personality and his historic role. In a shrewd appraisal of the Russian *melée symboliste* [29] he spoke of the " heroic activity of Valerii Briusov " as " an attempt to combine the principles of the French Parnassians and the dreams of the Russian Symbolists, a typical drama of will and environment, of personality and historic movement." [30]

Briusov's diary offers ample proof of an early resolve to reach the commanding heights of Russian literature and, in his own phrase quoted by Khodasevich, to " earn two lines in a history of world literature." When still a high-school senior he viewed a literary career as a challenge to be met, literary fame as a stronghold to be conquered. Several years before his studiously blatant debut which duly shocked the Philis-

---

[29] " Nekotorye techeniia v sovremennoi russkoi poèzii " [Some Trends in Contemporary Russian Poetry], *Apollon*, No. 1 (1913), pp. 46–50.

[30] *Ibid.*, p. 177.

tines, he committed to his diary [31] his ambition to ride the crest of the literary wave of the future. "Decadence," he said in an 1893 entry, "is surging ahead. It will prevail, especially when it finds a leader worthy of itself. And this leader will be I, yes, I!" [32] Coming from a boy of seventeen who was yet to appear upon the literary stage, this was a striking statement.

Yet this seemingly arrogant prophecy—or should one say, ambitious scheme?—was fully vindicated. Ten years later Briusov was the unchallenged head of the Russian Symbolist movement, especially of its Moscow wing, editor of the most influential Modernist journal *The Scales*, in a word, a legislator of the literary taste. How much his stewardship meant to his fellow Symbolists can be gleaned from the statement of one of the most brilliant among them, Andrei Belyi: "Briusov was for us the only *maître*, a fighter for all that was new, the organizer of propaganda; we subordinated ourselves to him as a leader and fighter. There was much that we knew about Briusov. But we kept it to ourselves, out of deference to his leadership." [33]

Clearly Briusov's ascendancy over his confreres could not have been entirely a matter of his superior organizational and promotional skills. In the years 1903–6 which witnessed the appearance of Briusov's most accomplished verses he was often acclaimed as the uncontested master of the modern Russian poetic idiom, as the leading poet in the land. These tributes, though grossly exaggerated, were not entirely undeserved. Briusov's prodigious industry and ever-widening literary culture, coupled with an incisive intelligence and some native poetic endowment, yielded an impressive image. His determination to absorb and to make his own the characteristic rhythms, strategies and attitudes of Russian modernism

[31] *Dnevniki [Diaries]*, 1891–1910 (Moscow, 1927).
[32] *Ibid.*, p. 12.
[33] Cf., *Sud'ba Bloka [Blok's Fate]*, ed. O. Nemerovskaia and Ts. Volpe (Leningrad, 1930), p. 65.

ushered in a number of poems so skillfully constructed, so ably orchestrated, so forcefully representative of the new sensibility as to be easily mistaken for masterpieces by some of **Briusov's** younger contemporaries, including poets finer than himself. Thus, after the publication of Briusov's widely acclaimed collection of verse, *Urbi et Orbi*, Aleksandr Blok, who was to develop into a lyrist of vastly superior suggestiveness and power, wrote reverently to his older colleague: "I have no hope of ever finding myself next to you. I do not purport to know if what is known to you will ever become available to the rest of us or to speculate as to how soon this is likely to happen." [34]

Eventually some of this wide-eyed adulation gave way to a more critical assessment of Briusov's strengths and weaknesses. In his fascinating "Reminiscences about A. A. Blok," [35] Belyi claims that Blok was " the first to realize that, that he [Briusov] is merely a mathematician, a calculator, a classifier and that there is no trace of a Magus in him." [36]

Blok's writings do not seem to yield quite so straightforward an expression of disenchantment with Briusov's vaunted "magic." Yet he seems to have struck a partly critical note in a letter to his friend and confidant Sergei Solov'ëv, written in January, 1905: "I do not understand anything about Briusov outside of the fact that he is the poet of genius of the Alexandrine period of Russian literature." [37] If the earlier overestimate of Briusov's poetic achievement persists in the extravagant phrase " of genius," the phrase " the Alexandrine period " may well represent a shrewd qualification.

In all fairness, in Blok's early Symbolist vocabulary "Alexandrine " was far from a derogatory term. In a homage to another fellow Symbolist, the learned and recondite Viacheslav

[34] *Ibid.*
[35] " Vospominaniia ob A. A. Bloke," *Epopeia*, No. 1 (Moscow–Berlin, 1921).
[36] Quoted in, *Sud'ba Bloka*, p. 65.
[37] *Ibid.*, p. 66.

Ivanov,[38] Blok spoke of the Symbolist age as the "Alexandrine" era in Russian letters, because of its two salient characteristics—a sense of imminent doom and a search for "broad cultural syntheses." It is fair to assume, however, that in using the adjective "Alexandrine" with reference to Briusov, Blok was not altogether unmindful of some of its usual implications, such as the emphasis on the eclectic, the anthological, the bookish, the proclivity for the derivative rather than the creative, the contrived rather than the natural.

This latter facet of the "Alexandrine" cluster becomes apparent in Briusov at a very early stage. In an 1892 poem written clearly under the influence of Arthur Rimbaud, Briusov declares:

I am a son of my age, a slave of our culture; / I do not care for torpid nature . . . I am not satisfied with truth and simplicity; / I vastly prefer the dreams of sickly poetry: / And the charms of a woman of artful beauty.[39]

Once again the *Zeitgeist* exacts a tribute. The eulogy of "sickly poetry" is part and parcel of the morbid sophistication of the self-consciously decadent era. Yet even in his stridently risqué verses which were designed to shock the literary conservatives, Briusov was a decadent with a difference. If at a later stage, in spite of all the dutifully cryptic references to the esoteric revelations allegedly embodied in the poet's "images, rhythms, words,"[40] Briusov's "magic" smacked to an intuitive contemporary of "mathematics," his gestures toward weary overrefinement were never convincing. Lassitude

---

[38] Cf., "Poèt i chern'" [The Poet and the Mob] (1905), A. Blok, *Sobranie sochinenii* [*Collected Works*] (Moscow–Leningrad, 1962), V, 7–18.

[39]   Я сын столетия, культуры нашей раб.
Не надо мне сияющей природы,
Мне мало истины, мне мало простоты!
Понятны мне мечты поэзии больной
И чары женщины с условной красотой.
(Quoted in, D. Maksimov, *Poèziia Valeriia Briusova*
[Leningrad, 1940], p. 28.)

[40] Briusov, *Izbrannye stikhotvoreniia*, p. 218.

and ennui were fundamentally alien to this energetic, imperious, hard-driven litterateur. He was much too curious and much too active to afford languor. His attitude toward the cultural heritage had none of the weary connoisseurship of one who " has read all the books "; it had the freshness of an avid learner and the vigor of a tireless explorer and *Kulturtraeger*. Culture to Briusov was not a source of rarefied thrills for a jaded palate, but an enormous body of tradition, a heterogeneous cluster of intellectual and technical skills to be learned, assimilated, mastered, and transmitted. Few Russian poets, if any, could vie with Briusov in his insatiable thirst for knowledge,[41] in his great, indeed indiscriminating, intellectual curiosity. In the course of his far-flung activity as poet, fiction writer, critic, and literary historian, he made the entire Western civilization his province. His sonnets, novels, and essays range over the vast expanse of cultural history, from classical antiquity through the Italian Renaissance and the German Reformation down to the latest trends or fads in French literature. Briusov's best work, I might add, testifies not only to the remarkably wide scope of his cultural receptivity, but to the vigor and relevance of his responses as well. His most distinguished novel, *The Fire Angel* (1907), set in sixteenth-century Germany, is a triumph of historical imagination.

In his already-cited memoir Khodasevich speaks of Briusov's intellectual "Don Juanism." The sexual metaphor is not altogether inappropriate. One sometimes has the feeling that Briusov's insatiable greed for culture was part of his appetite for experience. He hoarded values, artifacts, beliefs, and civilizations as he did "encounters," vigorously and indiscriminately, and he was no more prepared to commit himself to a single-value system than he was to any of the multifarious priestesses

---

[41] " Oh God! my God! " he once wrote. " Even if I could live a hundred lives, I still could not satisfy that thirst for knowledge which consumes me." *Valerii Briusov, in Autobiographical Notes, Letters, Reminiscences of Contemporaries*, ed. N. Ashukin (Moscow, 1929), p. 273.

with whom he happened to " celebrate the rite." History was to Briusov an extended pageant, an unfolding spectacle. In a characteristic poem " The Lanterns," [42] where Briusov reviews successive civilizations, Assyria, Egypt, India, Greece, Rome, Renaissance Italy, Luther's Germany, and the age of the French Revolution are likened to little lanterns, " now bright, now dim," gleaming in the darkness. All of these seem to have an equal appeal to the poet's fascinated gaze. Always prepared to celebrate anything that is or was, he is getting ready to hail what is going to be: " I pray to you, the yet unknown, the yet hidden in the shadows of the night, ye, flames of the future! " [43]

This ideational promiscuity is the leitmotiv of the culture-oriented verses of Briusov. In the much-quoted poem " I " (1899) he declares somewhat boastfully: " My spirit did not wane in the mist of contradictions / My mind did not flag amid fatal linkages / I love all dreams, all manners of speech are dear to me / And I dedicate my verse to all Gods." [44] To all Gods, and thus to none.

A subsequent quatrain of the same poem anticipates the defiantly aesthetic emphasis, indeed the phraseology, of " To the Poet ":

I visited the gardens of Lyceums and Academies. / I took down the wise men's dicta in wax / As a faithful disciple, I was caressed by all of them / As for me, *I loved only the combinations of words.* [45] [My italics.]

[42] Briusov, *Stephanos*, pp. 145–46.

[43] *Ibid.*, p. 146.

[44]   Мой дух не изнемог во мгле противоречий
          Не обессилел ум в сцепленьях роковых.
          Я все мечты люблю, мне дороги все речи,
              И всем богам я посвящаю стих.

                                    (Briusov, *Izbrannye stikhotvoreniia*, p. 56.)

[45]   Я посещал сады Ликеев, Академий,
          На воске отмечал реченья мудрецов,
          Как верный ученик, я был ласкаем всеми,
              Но сам любил лишь сочетанья слов.

                                                            (*Ibid.*)

Two years later in a poem addressed, not without a polemical intent, to that *grande dame* of Russian Symbolism, the poet-critic Zinaida Gippius, who combined vaguely decadent affectations with a hankering for a metaphysical "engagement," Briusov sounded again the note of freedom from entangling beliefs:

"An unshakeable truth / I have abandoned long ago / And all seas, all harbors / I love equally . . . I want my free boat / To roam everywhere / I wish to praise / The Lord and the Devil alike." [46]

What is implicit here, at least on the face of it, is a steadfast refusal to make a moral choice, indeed a professed aloofness from any criteria that might provide a viable basis for such a choice. The image of himself which Briusov is eager to project in his early and middle periods is that of a free-wheeling aesthete, an essentially amoral hedonist. While this self-image should not be taken too literally, the young Briusov was taking it seriously enough to jot down in his sparse, but often revealing, diary on April 22, 1894, the following phrase: "Sulla belonged to the same category as I. Those are gifted men *sans foi ni loi*, who live for pleasure alone." [47]

5.

Few Russian men of letters whose careers spanned the period between the two revolutions managed to escape the challenges

---

[46]   Неколебимой истине
      Не верю я давно,
И все моря, все пристани
      Люблю, люблю равно.

Хочу, чтоб всюду плавала
      Свободная ладья.
И господа и дьявола
      Хочу прославить я.
      (Valerii Briusov, *Stikhotvoreniia* [*Poems*] [Leningrad, 1953], p. 153.)
[47] Briusov, *Dnevniki* [*Diaries*], p. 156.

and temptations of political involvement. Since Briusov was the only major Russian Symbolist figure to join the Communist party after 1917 and to become an active supporter of the Bolshevik regime until his death, the Soviet literary historians have a vested interest in overstating the degree of Briusov's social awareness prior to the November coup. Actually, as D. S. Mirsky has demonstrated,[48] throughout much of his career Briusov's attitude toward politics, in line with his general stance, was thoroughly aesthetic. Most of Briusov's confreres were perceptibly affected by the events of 1905. The first Russian Revolution injected the note of heightened social concern, of vague moral uneasiness or upper-class guilt into the writings of Belyi and Blok. Even the admittedly narcissistic lyrist Balmont was drawn, be it for a moment, into the sphere of social protest. Briusov's reaction was essentially one of a "cold witness." (Such poems as "The Mason" which have been cited as instances of a sympathetic response to the revolutionary movement are primarily a matter of experimenting, briefly and inconclusively, with the "civic" manner, of proving to oneself and others that the *maître* could handle this style, too.)

In a letter to the well-known critic Kornei Chukovskii, Briusov sounds like a detached, self-involved litterateur: "From the historical point of view our Russian troubles may be necessary, from the aesthetic point of view, if contemplated at considerable distance, they are arresting, but to live in their midst is tedious!"[49] Since the appeal of history to the poet was primarily visual, the spectacular and the dramatic seemed vastly preferable to the drab and uneventful. Thus, the extremes of tyranny and revolutionary anarchy were adjudged superior to the bleak middle ground of moderation. "Beautiful in the splendor of his power is the Oriental king Assar-

---

[48] *A History of Russian Literature* (New York, 1949), p. 436.
[49] D. Maksimov, *Poèziia Valeriia Briusova*, p. 196.

haddon, and beautiful the ocean of a people's wrath beating to pieces a tottering throne. But hateful are half-measures."[50]

Soviet critics like to interpret Briusov's contemptuous references to the middle-of-the-road liberals as a symptom of his moving to the Left. This theory is considerably weakened by eyewitness testimony: Khodasevich cites some rather blatantly "reactionary" remarks made by Briusov between 1905 and 1918.[51] It is at least arguable that Briusov's hard-headedness made him wary of some liberal delusions. Yet his fundamental objections to the *Duma* moderates were aesthetic. Their parliamentarian quibbling failed to provide this insatiable spectator with a sufficiently exciting show.

In the light of this record, Briusov's enthusiastic acceptance of the Bolshevik regime may seem to be something of a freak. He was not the only Symbolist to hail the November revolution, but he went considerably further in his support of the new regime than did either Belyi or Blok. In his post-1917 collections of verse, *In Such Days* (1921), *The Moment* (1922), *Distances* (1922), and *Mea* (1924) he eulogized the universal sweep and the liberating mission of the proletarian revolution; ("You will shine above all the holy dates, you blinding October!");[52] he hailed the triumphal march of humanity from Pericles to Lenin; he was announcing *urbi et orbi* that "faithful to a dream / Russia was marching toward glorious victories at the helm of the tribes of the earth."[53] He sang paeans to Lenin's wise guidance and upon the leader's death joined the official mourners to intone a cliché-ridden requiem to Mozart's music: "Kneeling before the Leader's grave / We hail, we hail our Lenin!"[54]

The spectacle of the erstwhile aesthete trumpeting "the

---

[50] Mirsky, *A History of Russian Literature*, p. 436.
[51] Khodasevich, *Nekropol'*.
[52] Quoted in, Maksimov, *Poèziia Valeriia Briusova*, p. 270.
[53] Briusov, *Izbrannye stikhotvoreniia*, p. 315.
[54] *Ibid.*, p. 438.

glorious news about the proletariat" seems an incongruous one. To be sure, the newly found "engagement" was a far cry from the blatantly ideological insouciance of the 1899 poem "I." Yet the paradox may be more apparent than real. If Briusov's rapid adjustment to the "new realities" was an act of political opportunism, he was a genuine, indeed an enthusiastic opportunist. Briusov's philosophy of culture had made him peculiarly vulnerable to twentieth-century history-mongering. A power and success worshipper, he was psychologically ready to come to terms with any *fait accompli*, especially if the central fact of the present seemed likely to become the wave of the future. (While many of Briusov's fellow intellectuals darkly prophesied the imminent collapse of Lenin's "experiment," Briusov apparently must have concluded that the Soviet regime was there to stay.) Poetry of lost causes had little appeal for Briusov. He was quite prepared to consign it, in Trotsky's winged phrase, to "the dustbin of history."

Moreover, as Mirsky has shrewdly pointed out, it was precisely the absence of any previous ethical commitments that made it relatively easy for Briusov to accept those facets of the new order which repelled many of the prerevolutionary Russian intelligentsia. In confronting the arbitrariness and brutality of the Red terror, Briusov was not encumbered by humanitarian scruples or libertarian ideals. A sense of purpose, decisiveness, or for that matter ruthlessness, were to him the inextricable concomitants or attributes of strength. To be sure, Briusov lacked most of the positive motives which impelled some of his fellow writers to espouse the revolutionary cause. The conscience-stricken nobleman's sense of guilt vis-à-vis the masses, frenzied social utopianism, an impassioned rejection of the status quo, breathless eagerness for a total transformation of the world—all these attitudes meant little to Valerii Briusov. Yet the Bolshevik revolution and the regime which emerged from it could have appealed to the former Symbolist *maître* on other grounds. We will recall that in 1905 Briusov claimed to be equally attracted by the power of an oriental despot and the people's wrath challenging it. The November revolution and its aftermath treated Briusov to both spectacles. It is interesting to note that while most of the literary fellow-travelers of the Revolution, poets like Belyi and Blok, novelists like Boris Pilniak, were carried away by its elemental sweep, Briusov did not offer his full support to the new regime until it demonstrated its ability and determination to subdue the "people's wrath," to transform the revolutionary chaos into an increasingly autocratic cosmos and harness it to the leader's grand design. The triumph of organization over the principle of spontaneity (*stikhiinost*)—so dear to the heart of "flabby" liberals and democratic socialists—was bound to gain Briusov's assent and admiration.

But the primacy of discipline, the increasing efficacy of controls, was not the only aspect of the Bolshevik mentality and performance which Briusov must have found congenial. This tireless literary toiler was bound to respond positively to the Soviet regime's emphasis on work and productivity, to the Leninist drive against the traditionally Russian sloth, inertia, inefficiency—in a word, *Oblomovitis*. An indifferent Marxist and a still more dubious Socialist, Briusov had little affinity, one suspects, for the working-class mystique. But he was truly committed to the cult of work. His 1919 eulogy of labor is probably sincere, even if it is tediously conventional: "In the universe of words which sparkle and burn . . . there is no more sacred word than 'labor.' "[55] The circumstances which occasioned this effusion were new, but the sentiment was not. Eighteen years earlier, in *Urbi et Orbi*, Briusov had sounded a similar note: "Welcome, hard work! / Plough, shovel and pick-axe! / The drops of sweat are refreshing. / The arm is delightfully weary."[56]

---

[55] Briusov, *Stikhotvoreniia*, p. 425.
[56]   Здравствуй тяжкая работа,
    Плуг, лопата и кирка!

Characteristically enough, the imagery of hard physical labor looms large in Briusov's metapoetry, more specifically in verse dealing with his own creative process. As Marina Tsvetaeva pointedly observed, one would have to look far and wide for another poet that would cast his vision in the form of a "faithful ox."[57] "Forward my dream! My faithful ox! / Forward, willingly or unwillingly! / I am walking beside you, my whip is heavy, / I am toiling myself, so do not you lag behind."[58] Tsvetaeva is right: Briusov has the unique distinction of speaking of his inspiration in the accents of the Volga Boatmen's Song.

If Briusov could thus embark with relatively good conscience upon his collaboration with the Soviet authorities, the latter were in a dire need of his prestige and erudition, his impressive organizational and didactic skills. In the first years of the Revolution few literary figures of Briusov's authority and experience aligned themselves unequivocally on the side of the Bolshevik regime. Thus, the party leaders were not averse to offering Briusov responsible if not exactly policy-making positions. He promptly became involved in a far-flung pedagogical activity as professor at the University of Moscow and one of the pillars of the Institute of Art and Literature where his vast scholarship, especially his expert knowledge of Russian and general prosody, was proving a boon to serious students of literature. In addition, he assumed bureaucratic responsibilities as head of the literature division of the Soviet Commissariat of Education. It seems that Briusov gave himself to these

---

Освежают капли мота,
Ноет сладостно рука!

(Briusov, *Izbrannye stikhotvoreniia*, p. 105.)

[57] Tsvetaeva, *Proza*, p. 209.

[58] Вперед мечта, мой верный вол!
Неволей, если не охотой,
Я близ тебя, мой кнут тяжел,
Я сам тружусь, и ты работай!

(Quoted in, G. Lelevich, *V. Ia. Briusov* [Moscow–Leningrad, 1926], p. 85.)

duties with exemplary zeal, indeed with gusto. The "organization man" of Russian Symbolism had a singularly unpoetic affinity for committee work. Khodasevich notes acidly: "He loved to attend meetings, not only as chairman but as participant, with a passionate, indeed somewhat perverse, love. 'Motion,' 'amendment,' 'vote,' 'constitution,' 'clause'—these words were music to his ears."[59]

And yet it is safe to assume that in spite of all these gratifications Briusov's last years were none too happy. The somewhat grudging official recognition was no substitute for a vital relationship with his fellow writers, which was becoming increasingly difficult if not impossible to maintain. Briusov's loyalty to the Soviets had infuriated those of his former associates who scornfully rejected the November revolution. His bureaucratic mode of collaboration tended to estrange the erstwhile enthusiasts who by 1920 were dispirited and confused. Nor was he getting much aid or comfort from the literary Left. The most vocal and colorful poets in the Bolshevik camp, the Futurists or neo-Futurists, such as Maiakovskii or N. Aseev, insisted that "revolutionary content" presupposed "revolutionary form," that is, *avant-garde* techniques, bold verbal experimentation. They scoffed at Briusov's attempts to pour new wine into old bottles. The idea of celebrating the proletarian revolution in the fairly traditional meters and shopworn imagery of the Symbolist age was adjudged futile and preposterous.

Strictly speaking, the Futurist charges were not altogether fair. Though in some of Briusov's Bolshevik odes the discrepancy between the ultrarevolutionary tenor and the tired poetic clichés is very embarrassing indeed, the aging poet's literary conservatism should not be overestimated. Partly owing to his remarkable intellectual flexibility and sophisticated relativism in matters of versification, partly out of his determination to keep pace with shifting literary tides so as not to be

[59] Khodasevich, *Nekropol'*, p. 49.

outdistanced, Briusov as a critic showed more sympathy for
Futurist innovations than did any of his fellow Symbolists,
with the possible exception of Andrei Belyi. As a practitioner
he bravely sought to absorb some of the *avant-garde* devices
by extending his earlier experiments with inexact rhymes, by
trying out various metrical patterns. Out of deference to what
he felt to be the spirit of the New age, he labored to couch
his metaphors in a cosmic, scientific vein. (This, incidentally,
was not a totally new emphasis: some fifteen years earlier,
when still editor of *The Scales*, Briusov featured prominently
in his journal an abortive attempt by an obscure French Symbolist, René Ghil, at " scientific poetry.")

Yet none of these strenuous efforts could save the bulk of
Briusov's post-1917 verse from vaporousness, stodginess, in a
word, sterility. These polished but lifeless poetic exercises were
produced in a vacuum. No one seemed to need them. They
were too blatantly propagandistic and " conformist " for the
unreconstructed intelligentsia, too conventional for the literary
radicals, too learned and recondite, too cluttered up by the
" archaistic " bric-a-brac of historical erudition (Maksimov)
to be accessible to the workers and peasants to whom Briusov's
" Bolshevik " poetry was allegedly addressed.

It would be a simplification to attribute the glaring weaknesses of Briusov's late verses to his inability to find an appropriate poetic pitch for his political " engagement." Symptoms
of creative exhaustion had been apparent in his poetry well
before 1917. As a lyrist Briusov reached his peak at the age of
thirty-five, during the heyday of the literary school which he
led so ably and forcefully. Perhaps, this " organizer of propaganda," this " leader and fighter " was too closely bound up
with the inner dynamism of the movement to be able to survive
its disintegration without losing much of his initial poetic
thrust.

It is an interesting commentary on the nature and limits of
Briusov's endowment that, in retrospect, the least vulnerable

aspect of his legacy is the one which depends less on poetic imagination than on analytical intelligence. Briusov's most enduring contribution, I believe, lies not in his lyric verse or, with the significant exception of *The Fire Angel*, in his artistic prose, but in his literary criticism which encompasses many perceptive, well-documented and closely argued reexaminations of the Russian literary masters. In his most effective poetry he expressed the literary *ambiance* of the age with competence and authority such as to earn him those "two lines in the history of world literature" for which he toiled so strenuously. Yet it is possible to argue that, except for a few truly memorable poems, be it the apocalyptic "Pale Horse" (*Kon' bled*) or the sharply etched mythological vignettes "The Eternal Truth of the Idols" (*Pravda vechnaia kumirov*), even the best of Briusov's poetry is often impressively second-rate. The virtues found here, e.g., sonority, eloquence, lucidity of the poetic argument, are many, but they are rhetorical rather than lyrical. What is missing time and again is "magic"—the haunting suggestiveness of the finest Symbolist verse, let alone the stunning verbal discoveries of the best post-Symbolist poets, of Mandelshtam, Maiakovskii, Pasternak. It is true that Briusov's reputation as a poet may suffer unduly from the contemporary reader's impatience with the hieratic and abstract quality of the turn-of-the-century vocabulary. Yet it is an earmark of a major poet to be able to survive the clichés of his age. Mallarmé, Rimbaud, Verlaine at his best, Blok and Belyi (especially as prose writer) speak to us above and beyond the vagaries of the Symbolist era. Briusov the poet remains primarily a purveyor of well-wrought period pieces.

A less than enthusiastic contemporary critic, Iurii Eichenwald, has called Briusov the "Salieri of modern Russian poetry." He was taking his cue, to be sure, from Pushkin's little tragedy "Mozart and Salieri," built around the contrast between the natural genius and the painstaking, plodding craftsman. The dictum was not designed to please Briusov and there is some evidence that he resented it deeply.[60] Yet while Eichenwald's intent was largely malicious, the simile need not be viewed simply as a dig at the mechanical, unspontaneous, deliberate quality of Briusov's poetic attainment. The profound dedication to literary craft—which Pushkin's Salieri protests a bit too stridently—was the chief source of Briusov's circumscribed and yet undeniable strength. Though at times an insufficient substitute for ethics, it was in itself a moral principle of some efficacy for it insured a high standard of professional integrity and that sturdy sense of responsibility for literary endeavor in Russia which was one of the finest traits of Briusov the editor, the critic, the teacher. Throughout his versatile career he was sustained, as Poggioli correctly observes, by the belief in what Mallarmé in his tribute to the memory of Théophile Gautier called "*la gloire ardente du métier.*"[61]

It is fitting that the name of Gautier be invoked, along with that of Mallarmé, in this closing phase of our story. Though Briusov's debt to the Flaubert–Mallarmé tradition is undeniable, his brand of aestheticism shows at least as much affinity for the flamboyant Romantic Bohemian Gautier as it does for the austere *maître* of French symbolism. He was an indefatigable craftsman, but ultimately not a purist. He was too energetic, too mundane, too sensuous, too power-minded to shun the direct gratifications, the temptations and pitfalls of the life of action. Perhaps, when all is said and done, "craft" was not for Briusov a strictly aesthetic category. It was rather a generic notion, a principle applicable to life and art alike, though especially operative in the latter, notably one of shaping, molding, transforming recalcitrant matter, bending the nonhuman to human purposes, asserting the primacy of intelligence and skill, the superiority of culture to nature. In Tsvetaeva's words, "Briusov came into this world to show what the Will can and cannot do, but primarily what it can do."[62] Few of

[60] *Ibid.*   [61] Poggioli, *Poets of Russia*, p. 105.   [62] Tsvetaeva, *Proza*, p. 214.

those familiar with Briusov's achievement will deny that on both counts the demonstration was an instructive one.

6.

If Briusov was the poet of the ego, Aleksandr Blok's infinitely more poignant and haunting legacy seems to be the triumph of the lyrical id. For Briusov the key term was self-discipline; for Blok—abandonment, surrender to forces beyond one's control. It is surely no accident that in Briusov's metapoems the commanding image is that of a steady hand wielding a whip or a shovel; in Blok's utterances about the poet the chief organ is the uncannily keen ear, the principal faculty—that of " listening " raptly to the inward music of the individual or collective soul. "What is a poet? " Blok asked in his diary. "A man who writes in verse? No, of course not. A poet is a carrier of rhythm." [63]

Few literary movements have encompassed two more disparate creative personalities than those of Valerii Briusov and Aleksandr Blok. For Briusov sacrifice meant ascetic self-control; for Blok, actual self-immolation. Moreover, what to the former was in large measure a piece of literary rhetoric became for the latter the central reality, the leitmotiv of that " emerging myth " of the poet (*tvorimaia legenda*, as Sologub has put it) which was to be revealed or prefigured by his poetry.

Because of the poignantly personal, indeed confessional, tone of Blok's verse it was traditionally viewed as a post-factum expression or transcript of the author's actual experiences. Yet one often has the feeling that the causal connection was in fact the reverse. Many a poem of Blok seems to have served as a literary scenario to be acted out in real life. Was Oscar Wilde's

[63] Quoted in, F. D. Reeve, *Aleksandr Blok: Between Image and Idea* (New York, 1962).

extravagant notion of life imitating art thus vindicated? Not
exactly. It would be more accurate to say, I believe, that life
and art alike were shaped here by a third force, the myth of
the artist as a tragic hero, as a dedicated custodian of "music."

It is a matter of record that for many of Blok's contemporaries his richly orchestrated poetry was overshadowed by
the mask of the man behind it. The late Boris Eichenbaum,
one of the finest Russian critics of the century, spoke for the
bulk of his generation when he said in 1921 in the wake of
Blok's untimely death: "For us Blok became a tragic actor
who played himself. . . . His youthful figure has fused with
his poetry in the same way in which the makeup of a tragic
actor is inseparable from his monologue. Each time Blok appeared before us, we felt a shiver down our spines. So much did
he resemble himself." [64]

At the height of his career Blok complained to his mother
that "vocation and authenticity are incompatible." The poet's
calling and the public role it imposed destroyed privacy. The
creator's personal life was turned into a lyrical drama enacted
against the appropriately eerie background of fog- and blizzard-
ridden St. Petersburg. The lovers of Russian poetry, the habitués, the hangers-on, watched with bated breath Blok's tem-
pestuous "encounters," participating vicariously in their hero's
—or, as an American critic recently put it,[65]—"scape-hero's"
desperate search for emotional fulfillment, a quest whose successive phases were embodied in such lyrical cycles as "Verses
About the Fair Lady" (1901–2), "The City" (1904–8), "The
Snow Mask" (1907), "The Terrible World" (1909–16).

How stringent were in Blok's view the demands of the vocation upon the man behind the poem can be gleaned from his
revealing "Letters on Poetry" (1908):

---

[64] "Sud'ba Bloka" [Blok's Fate], *Skvoz' literaturu* [*Across Literature*] (Leningrad,
1924), pp. 217, 219.

[65] The term is used by Leslie Fiedler in his recent book, *Love and Death in the
American Novel* (New York, 1960).

Only that which was the writer's confession, only that literary creation in which the author *burned himself to ashes* can achieve greatness. [My italics.] If the soul immolated thus is enormous, it will move more than one generation, one people, one country. But even if the soul is not great, sooner or later it will move at last the poet's contemporaries, not by his craft or originality but by the sincerity of his self-sacrifice.[66]

Let us note the difference between Blok's phrase "burned himself to ashes" and Briusov's "your cheeks like Dante's must be scorched by subterranean fire." Briusov urges a controlled experiment, a surface exposure to pain as one of the many dimensions of human existence to be investigated. To Blok the poet's compelling urge, as well as moral obligation, is a readiness to give himself, come what may, to elemental forces which, in a French phrase are "*plus fort que moi*," to be overpowered by an emotional or societal blizzard. The wind which in the opening passage of Blok's famous poem of the Revolution, "The Twelve," "sweeps you off your feet" is the leitmotiv of his life and work.[67]

"Elements" (*stikhiia*) and "music" were key terms in the vocabulary of Aleksandr Blok as poet and essayist, and they were often used almost interchangeably. Since Verlaine's whimsical "*Art Poétique*" *la musique* had been the watchword of the Symbolist movement. Yet in Blok and some other Russian Symbolists this slogan acquired a special emotional urgency. What to Verlaine was primarily a literary postulate, a metaphor for a wider range of poetic suggestiveness, an ineffable lyrical essence which traditional literary rhetoric could neither

[66] A. Blok, "Pis'ma o poèzii," *Sobranie sochinenii* [*Collected Works*] (Moscow–Leningrad, 1962), V, 278.

[67] Pasternak's recent lyrical triptych dedicated to Blok's memory and characteristically entitled "The Wind" contains the following lines:

> This wind we know is everywhere—at home,
> In trees and in the villages, in rain
> Or in his poetry's third volume
> Or in *The Twelve*, and then in death again.

(Boris Pasternak, *In the Interlude, Poems 1945–1960* [London, 1962], p. 155.)

capture nor convey, was to Blok a moral imperative. When the Russian poet spoke of music, and he did so time and again, he meant not so much a quality inherent in the poem as a way of life, an existential commitment to living dangerously, at the highest pitch of consuming emotional intensity. In his much quoted harangue "The Intelligentsia and the Revolution," a prose companion piece of "The Twelve," Blok was pleading with his fellow intellectuals who were either aloof from or hostile to the Bolshevik revolution: "But the spirit is Music. Daemon once told Socrates to listen to the spirit of music. With every cell of your body, with all your heart, with all your consciousness listen to the Revolution!" [68]

Nine years earlier in an essay "The Soul of a Writer" Blok insisted that the earmark of a literary artist is the incessantly intent inward hearing, the ability to listen to a distant music.[69] The writer can afford to "play" only if he knows his own rhythm and is attuned to the music of the world orchestra. On February 11, 1913, he wrote in his diary: "The morality of the world is unfathomable and quite different from what is usually meant by this word. What makes the world go round is music, passion, prejudice, power." [70] The same note was sounded in one of the latest entries: "In the beginning was Music. Music is the world's essence. Culture is the musical rhythm through which the world grows." [71]

These persistent intimations were borne out by Blok's life as actually lived and as stylized in his lyrical verse. The driving force of this *agon* is the view of poetry as an act of total (i. e., rapt, unceasing, strenuous) listening to elemental rhythms surging below, a view in which the spirit of music and the motif of self-sacrifice are fused organically. The bulk of Blok's poetic achievement adds up to a *sui generis* passion play about the

[68] Blok, *Sobranie sochinenii*, VI, 20.
[69] *Ibid.*, V, 370–71.
[70] Quoted in, K. Mochulskii, *Aleksandr Blok* (Paris, 1948), p. 384.
[71] Quoted in, Helen Muchnic, *From Gorky to Pasternak* (New York, 1961), p. 177.

poet's self-imposed ordeal. The three acts of the drama correspond to three successive phases of the chief protagonist's never-ending search for salvation.

The fundamental landmarks on Blok's road to Calvary have been repeatedly identified by both Russian and Western literary scholars, e. g., K. Mochulskii, C. M. Bowra, S. Bonneau, Janko Lavrin, H. Muchnic.[72] "The Fair Lady," "The Stranger" and "The Native Land" sequences, held together as each of them is by the unity of the love object, can be said to represent respectively: a) seraphic innocence, b) self-destructive, Dionysian eroticism and, c) an ambivalent, guilt-ridden involvement with Russia's national destiny.

It is essential to note that at each juncture we are dealing with erotic poetry, though the target varies drastically from period to period. The theme of love, or rather of being-in-love remains constant. "Infatuation," a very inadequate English equivalent of *vliublennost'*, is characteristically one of Blok's favorite words. It serves as the title for two poems written during his middle period. The mistily romantic 1905 poem whose opening line is "The princess lived on a high mountain," proclaims being-in-love as the poet's destiny, the law governing his life:

> O Infatuation, you are sterner than Fate!
> More imperious than the ancient laws of our
>   fathers!
> Sweeter than the sound of the trumpet! [73]

The heroine of Blok's first lyrical cycle "Verses About the Fair Lady" is an epitome of Goethe's eternally feminine, or

---

[72] Mochulskii, *Aleksandr Blok*; C. M. Bowra, *The Heritage of Symbolism* (London, 1943); Sophie Bonneau, *L'univers poétique d'Alexandre Blok* (Paris, 1946); Janko Lavrin, *From Pushkin to Mayakovsky* (London, 1948); Muchnic, *From Gorky to Pasternak.*

[73]   О Влюбленность! Ты строже судьбы!
    Повелительней древних законов отцов!
    Слаще звуков военной трубы!

(Blok, *Sobranie sochinenii*, II, 62.)

more immediately, an image suggested by that influential philosopher-poet, Vladimir Solovëv whose cult of Sophia, the female embodiment of the Divine Wisdom, had made a profound impact at the beginning of the century upon the young Symbolist seers. This esoteric beloved appears in Blok's early verse within a fairy-tale setting, now as a mysterious maiden, now as a princess living in an enchanted castle upon a snow-capped mountain peak. Whatever the guise, she is invariably exalted, inaccessible—a legend rather than a blood-and-flesh woman, an object of timid adoration and futile longing. All that remains to the younger worshipper is to burn incense and to wait for a miracle.

The tenor of this disembodied love poetry is one of enraptured anticipation of "love and agony":

> I have forebodings of thee.
> Time is going
> I fear for all that in thy face I see
> The sky's aflame, intolerably glowing
> Silent I wait in love and agony.[74]

The fear which we detect in these lines is not one of rejection, of being spurned by the Fair Lady, if and when she deigns to appear, but of disenchantment or betrayal. It is a metaphysical, a religious doubt. The vague yet insidious presentiment that the long-awaited encounter would lead to a tragic letdown may well have been a projection of the poet's growing sense of his own unworthiness and corruptibility:

> How I shall fall! How sorrowful and lowly,
> Unmastered all my mortal fantasies!

---

[74] The translation is drawn from C. M. Bowra, *A Book of Russian Verse* [London, 1943], p. 97.

Предчувствую Тебя. Года проходят мимо—
Все в облике одном предчувствую Тебя.
Весь горизонт в огне—и ясен нестерпимо,
И молча жду,—тоскуя и любя.

(Blok, *Sobranie sochinenii*, I, 94.)

The sky's aflame, draws nigh thy splendor holy,
But it is strange, thy look will change on thee.[75]

Blok's apprehension was borne out. The face of the Fair Lady
has indeed changed. The star has fallen. A mysterious maiden
has become a stranger, apparently a demimondaine, still elusive, but by now tarnished, ambiguous, if not sinful. In such
cycles as "The City," and later, "The Terrible World," the
landscape of the poet's soul undergoes a drastic transformation. The medieval ballad-like settings are supplanted by
sordid, tawdry, urban imagery—"taverns, by-streets, electric
nightmares"[76] of a vice-ridden, teeming metropolis.

Apparently the quivering innocence of the first period could
not be sustained. In the process of a painful maturation of the
man and the poet, the adolescent worship of the Fair Lady had
to give way to a more complex and tragic vision of life and love
where mysticism alternates with blatant realism, intermittent
bliss of being-in-love with blasphemous irony and self-mockery,
Dionysian intoxication with a spiritual hangover. The moments
of total surrender to a dark passion, of a near-complete break-
down of ego controls, at once irresistibly tempting and terri-
fying, are objectified in one of Blok's most haunting poems, in
an image of a charger racing across a bottomless pit:

> In a light heart—passion and insouciance,
> As if a signal were given us from the sea,
> Over a bottomless drop into eternity
> Breathless a charger races.[77]

---

[75]   О, как паду—и горестно и низко,
Не одолев смертельныя мечты!
Как ясен горизонт! И лучезарность близко.
Но страшно мне: изменишь облик Ты.

(Ibid.)

[76] Blok, *Sobranie sochinenii*, II, 159.
[77]   В легком сердце—страсть и беспечность,
Точно с моря нам подан знак,
Над бездонным провалом в вечность
Задыхаясь, летит рысак.

(Ibid., III, 162.)

The aftermath is apathy, stupor, self-disgust: "I'm chained to a tavern. I've been drunk for a long time. I do not care." "Is this what we have called love?"[78]

Was it the inherent dualism of Blok's psyche—the Dmitri Karamazov-like oscillation between "the ideal of the Madonna" and "the ideal of Sodom" that drove Blok into that gypsy whirlpool, that orgiastic, self-destructive eroticism? Whatever the emotional urges underlying the behavior of Aleksandr Blok, the protagonist of Blok's lyrical drama, the matter transcends the merely personal. Once again, the causal relationship between *Dichtung* and *Wahrheit* is more complex than some literary historians seem to realize.

As Viktor Zhirmunskii has pointed out in what is still the best single essay on Blok's poetry,[79] the motive force of the autobiographical spectacle whose main phases I am trying to reconstruct here was "spiritual maximalism," an all-or-nothing moral frenzy which, in Blok's view, was a trademark, indeed the destiny of a true poet. Zhirmunskii points out correctly that in spite of Blok's frequent falls during the "Terrible World" era, in spite of all the blasphemies and the moments of nihilistic despair, his metaphysical hunger never abated. "I seek salvation," declared Blok in a poem written in 1900, in the course of his seraphic apprenticeship. He was still seeking salvation; he was still reaching toward the miracle as he plumbed the depths of frantic sensuality whose very intensity seemed to promise an emotional breakthrough, a climactic thrill, an ultimate experience. To be sure, the price of the search was extravagantly high. The "fallen angel," as Aleksei Tolstoy has called him, was burning himself to ashes. The feverish promiscuity destroyed whatever peace of mind he was capable of achieving and undermined beyond repair his self-respect. But then was not self-destruction the inexorable test of the poet's sincerity and the cost of his greatness?

[78] *Ibid.*, pp. 31, 168.
[79] *Poeziia Aleksandra Bloka* (Petrograd, 1922).

Yet this phase could not last indefinitely either. "Terrible world!," cried the poet in a 1910 lyric, "You are too narrow for the heart!" [80] History was knocking at the door of the self-involved poet. The "tragic tenor of the era" (A. Akhmatova) was suffocating in the sultry eroticism of gypsy restaurants. He needed an escape from lyrical isolation, a way out of narcissism into the wide open spaces of a great national theme. Thus a new myth is born, and with it a new lyrical cycle, "The Native Land" (1907–16). In 1908 a new feminine symbol starts haunting Blok's poetry, now alternating with, now superseding, a Carmen or a Mary. Her name is Russia. Georgii Adamovich, the dean of Russian *émigré* critics, observed judiciously [81] that Blok's Russia was a metaphysical entity rather than a cultural or political actuality. One might add that in Blok's verse, "The Native Land"—be it the "beggared Russia," "the drunken Russia," or "my fatal country"—is an idiosyncratic, personal myth or, to put it differently, another female protagonist in Blok's lyrical drama, another object of a fervid and ambivalent passion.

7.

In Blok's early verses the motif of Russia appears within a quasi-Slavophile *ambiance*. "Rus'" is an epitome of purity, an object of reverence—in short, a Fair Lady writ large. Yet the heroine of Blok's civic poems in the decade immediately preceding the Revolution is neither the radiant maiden nor the traditional "Mother Russia." Instead, she is a wife ("O Russia, my wife, our path is painfully clear!") [82] or, more frequently, an ardent wild mistress, a Carmen with Tartar eyes.

[80] Blok, *Sobranie sochinenii*, III, 163.
[81] *Odinochestvo i svoboda* [*Solitude and Freedom*] (New York, 1955).
[82] "Na pole Kulikovom" [On the Kulikovo Field] III, 249.

Not unlike Gogol or Tiutchev, Blok is irresistibly drawn to Russia thus stylized in spite of, if not because of, her failings. The murky romance can be strained yet it will not be destroyed either by Russia's bleakness and poverty—qualities which the mid-nineteenth-century Slavophiles hailed as proof positive of their country's truly Christian essence—or, for that matter, by the tawdry or meretricious traits which the image of the native land occasionally displays.[83] At times the poet seems to chafe at the bit as he rails against the savagery and primitivism of his accursed lover. ("Russia, my life, are we doomed to a common fate . . . What use is your darkness to a free soul?") Yet the revolt remains futile and short-lived. The fatal bond will not be broken. For one thing, the very darkness, so abhorrent to the poet's "free soul," holds an irresistible attraction to his id—the irrational, Dionysian, self-destructive facet of his psyche. For another thing, the Symbolist poet's determination to listen, whatever the cost, to the discordant music of the elements is compounded here by an acute sense of social responsibility strongly tinged with an upper-class sense of guilt vis-à-vis the people.

This anguished social awareness assumed an increasingly important role in Blok's writings during the last pre-revolutionary decade, especially in his controversial essays and lectures. In "The Intelligentsia and the People," "The Elements and Culture," "Three Questions,"[84] he keeps sounding the same dark warning. The world in which we live is a castle built on sand. The Russian intellectual dwells in a fool's paradise: his sheltered world is precarious and doomed.

The intelligentsia and the people, argued Blok, are facing each other across an unbridgeable chasm. When the long

---

[83] See especially, the 1914 poem whose opening lines, in Babette Deutsch's translation, are "To sin unshamed, to lose unthinking / count of careless nights and days . . ." (*A Treasury of Russian Verse*, ed. A. Yarmolinsky [New York, 1949], pp. 153–54).

[84] "Intelligentsiia i narod," "Stikhiia i kul'tura," "Tri voprosa," *Sobranie sochinenii*, V, 233–40; 318–28; 350–59.

pent-up resentment of the inert, sullen masses finally erupts, the world of the intelligentsia will go down in flames. Harking back to the famous passage in Gogol's *Dead Souls* whose imagery was to reverberate through Blok's impassioned harangues, he inquired in anguish, "And what if the *troika races at us?* [My italics.] What if in reaching toward the people, we throw ourselves under the hooves of a furious troika which is out to destroy us?" [85] And he added ominously, "Perhaps the darkness within which we dwell is due to the fact that the horse's hairy chest is already hanging over us, and his heavy hooves are ready to descend?" [86]

These Cassandra-like utterances stirred a lively controversy among the Russian literary elite. The acid poet-critic, Zinaida Gippius spoke somewhat disparagingly of Blok's cryptic stammering. Fëdor Sologub, one of the older Symbolist poets and a distinguished novelist, opined: "Blok is wise when he writes verse, but he is not so wise when he attempts to write prose." D. S. Filosofov, a close associate of Merezhkovskii, accused Blok of self-hatred: "Blok," he argued rather shrewdly, "is tired of his own sophistication." [87]

These criticisms were not altogether unwarranted. Clearly the discursive mode was not Blok's forte. His natural element was music rather than logic. In precision, rigor and cogency Blok's expository prose was vastly inferior to Briusov's, Ivanov's or Belyi's in his most sober moments. In fact, Blok could not effectively argue with his opponents since even as an essayist he dealt in lyrical metaphors rather than in concepts. He could merely project a mood, a stance, a vague presentiment.

Yet this was only part of the story. On balance, some of the literati may have been a bit too hasty or complacent in rejecting his urgent message. The author of "The Twelve" was not a sustained thinker, but he was admittedly a superb listener. His single-minded dedication to music entailed an uncanny

[85] *Ibid.*, p. 328.   [86] *Ibid.*   [87] *Ibid.*, V, 721.

alertness to the rhythms of history. In Blok, the faculty which Lionel Trilling has called the "imagination of disaster" was developed to the highest possible degree. No poet of the Silver age gave a more striking expression to the "ever-present sense of catastrophe," the brooding anticipation of an impending cataclysm. This is not to say that Blok's contemporaries failed to share his half-hopeful, half-fearful premonitions. Belyi's brilliant novel *St. Petersburg* is permeated with an apocalyptic sense of doom. In a different, somewhat Spenglerian vein, Briusov's poem "The Coming Huns" prefigures an imminent barbarian flood that is to engulf Western civilization. Yet clearly this was not a kind of insight with which a literary generation could live most of the time. To construe the dazzling esotericity of the Russian Symbolist elite as a mode of intellectual escapism would be an inexcusably gross simplification. But to many an observer the feverish intensity with which abstruse metaphysical and aesthetic questions were debated at the famous Wednesday evenings at the Ivanovs' or at the sessions of the Religious-Philosophical Society must have smacked of an ideational "feast during the plague." This, for better or for worse, was Blok's response to much of the Silver age intellection. Though a man of wide literary culture and of broad intellectual interests, he was not enough of a professional *littérateur* or metaphysician to feel at home in the rarefied atmosphere of those symposia which ranged from Oscar Wilde to Nietzsche, from Eleusinian mysteries to neo-Kantian philosophy. The more intently he listened to the elemental rhythms surging below, the more likely he was to view the finespun talk of his confreres as a matter of recondite fiddling while Rome is about to burn.

There is an essential difference—and it is one which in our century is often overlooked—between recognizing the overwhelming likelihood of an historical process and acquiescing in it, or, more relevantly, abdicating one's right to moral judgment vis-à-vis the "inevitable." Yet this was precisely what Blok proceded to do on the eve of World War I: "What flame will burst from beneath this crust—a pernicious or a salutary one? And will we have the right to say that this flame is pernicious if all it is going to destroy is us, the intelligentsia? "[88]

There is in this query a shattering candor so characteristic of Blok, a heroic determination to reach beyond vested interests and the self-serving parochialism of literary coteries, indeed beyond mere self-preservation, toward larger truths and a wider ideal of social justice. But there is also in it, I believe, an excessive readiness for moral self-effacement or self-denial, for surrendering one's own values to the inexorable historical process, an *amor fati* so typical of the modern intellectual with a bad conscience. "Who am I," inquires Blok in effect, "to stand in the way of history? Who am I, the son of a privileged class, to judge the first acts of the awakening masses? Is the destruction of my own group, of my artificial, hothouse way of life too high a price to be paid for overdue social change? "

To admire the selflessness of this sacrificial gesture is not necessarily to be uncritical of Blok's ideological position. Whatever the failings of the Russian intelligentsia—and these were many—it was a moral order rather than a guild or a coterie. Today it is difficult not to see what Blok's sense of social guilt as well as a morbid fascination with doom prevented him from seeing, notably that the destruction of the prerevolutionary intelligentsia was to spell a major loss to Russian culture, Russian society and indeed, the very Russian people in whose behalf the sacrifice was to be made.

There is an element of irony in Blok's impassioned dialogue with his contemporaries. A visionary in quest of a miracle, of a personal salvation, an introspective lyrist who saw in poetry primarily a projection and a vehicle of a unique creative personality,[89] Blok was the very epitome of Romantic individualism. Yet few of his programmatic essays written during the

---

[88] *Ibid.*, p. 121.
[89] See especially, Blok's essay " O lirike " [On Lyric Poetry], *Sochineniia*, V, 130–61.

fear- and hope-ridden decade of 1908–18 fail to contain a scathing attack on the individualistic fallacy.

Is it necessary to urge that this apparent contradiction was fully consistent with Blok's notion of the artist's calling? If, as he argued in his 1908 essay, "the poet's soul must move the contemporaries by the sincerity of his self-sacrifice," is not the creator's sacred duty to renounce his supreme values, to deny himself the satisfaction of his fundamental emotional and ideational needs? The motif of self-immolation acquires a special poignancy on the eve of the Revolution when Blok declares his readiness to surrender unconditionally the rarefied culture, of which he was one of the finest products, to the elemental rhythms of an imminent cataclysm.

This attitude finds a striking expression in "The Twelve" (1918), probably the most remarkable poetic response to the Bolshevik Revolution. The opening passage of the poem with its commanding image of the world-wide blizzard conveys the cosmic sweep of Blok's eschatological vision:

> Black evening,
> White snow!
> The wind, the wind
> Across God's world it blows! [90]

Let us briefly recall the plot of this much-praised, much-maligned poem. In a pitch-black night twelve Red militiamen patrol the streets of beseiged, blizzard-swept Petrograd. These guardians of the new order present a none too edifying spectacle. They abuse their firepower to settle personal quarrels. They join with the hoodlums in pillaging the cellars of the

---

[90]   Черный вечер,
Белый снег!
·   ·   ·   ·   ·   ·

Ветер, ветер
На всем божьем свете!

(Blok, *Sochineniia*, III, 347.)

"*bourgeoisie.*" They bully the pathetic relics of the "ancient regime." They are brutes, primitives blinded by hate as they are, literally, by the snow which the wind throws in their faces, a grim demolition squad incapable of visualizing, let alone performing, any constructive tasks. And yet in the grand finale no less a figure than Jesus Christ floating high above the snow appears at the head of the sinister procession. It is He who leads the twelve apostles with bloodstained hands, without their knowledge, indeed, perhaps, against their will, toward a *vita nuova*, toward an infinitely "beautiful life." [91]

In the already quoted essay—"The Intelligentsia and the Revolution"—in which Blok stridently urged his fellow intellectuals to listen to the music of the Revolution, the poet was celebrating the readiness of the new era to "transform everything, so that our deceitful, filthy, dull and ugly life could become just, pure, joyous and beautiful." "The artist's job," he urged, "the artist's duty, is to see what is intended, to listen to that music which thunders in the 'wind torn to shreds.'" [92] . . . "The only way to live is to make boundless demands on life; to believe in what must be . . . For life will give us back all this, because it is beautiful." [93] This leap of utopian faith is bound up characteristically with another outburst of upper-class guilt feeling: "The estates are burning, cultural treasures are pillaged by vandals, but what right do we have to complain?" . . . "We are links in a chain. Are we not weighed down by our fathers' sins?" [94]

It is impossible to understand "The Twelve" unless one sees this poem as the high point of the "Russia" cycle, a culmination of Blok's entire poetic and spiritual evolution, or the last act of a lyrical drama rather than a political manifesto. In

[91] See fn. 93.
[92] The last words, of course, are drawn from the finale of Part I of *Dead Souls.* Gogol's romantic hyperboles serve here, not inappropriately, as a vehicle for Blok's Utopian fervor.
[93] Blok, *Sobranie sochinenii*, VI, 12.
[94] *Ibid.*, p. 15.

spite of Blok's indubitable social concern and his acute sense
of history, the images, the symbols, the essential spiritual thrust
and texture of his poetry belong to a sphere fundamentally
different from, though occasionally overlapping with, that of
politics. Blok remarked on this often, sometimes with a tinge
of apology and bafflement. In an introduction to his narrative
poem, " The Retribution " he says: " The winter of 1911 was
full of profound internal tension and anxiety. I remember long
conversations through the night during which there emerged
the impossibility to either separate or blend art, life and politics." [95] In 1905 he wrote to his father: " I'll never become a
revolutionary or a ' builder of life,' not because I fail to see the
validity of the one or the other but in view of the nature,
quality and subject matter of my inward experiences." [96]
Twelve years later—on the eve of the Bolshevik coup—he was
confessing his inability to make political choices, his confusion
and helplessness in the realm of political action: " I will never
reach for power; I'll never join a party, I'll never make a choice.
I have nothing to be proud of. I don't understand anything." [97]
Clearly, the subject matter of Blok's inner life was a far cry
from tangible political realities. Blok's Revolution, that purifying cosmic blizzard presided over by Jesus Christ bears no
more resemblance to the Revolution of 1917 than does the
Russia of his earlier poems to the pre-1914 tsarist empire.
In either case we are confronted with a " metaphysical entity,"
a personal myth.

Yet, at moments such as 1918, as Blok put it a few years
earlier, art and politics can neither be fused nor separated. It
was inevitable that " The Twelve " should have become the
focus of a vehement political controversy. The strange alliance
of Jesus Christ with the Bolshevik revolution shocked nearly
everyone. The Marxist-Leninists were puzzled and displeased

[95] *Ibid.*, III, 296.
[96] *Sud'ba Bloka,* ed. Nemerovskaia and Volpe, p. 91.
[97] *Ibid.*, p. 213.

by 'the unexpected ending of the poem, even if it seemed to epitomize the ultimate apotheosis of the revolutionary violence. The anti-Bolshevik intellectuals (e. g., Dmitrii Merezhkovskii and Zinaida Gippius), were still more acrimonious. They seized upon the opening section of the poem which parades the ineffectual relics of the *ancien régime*, especially upon the unflattering portrayal of the somberly intransigent litterateur, to accuse Blok of having sold out to the powers that be. In this understandable, if somewhat misguided indignation the detractors of " The Twelve " seemed to have lost sight of an important structural characteristic of the poem. Unlike " The Scythians " (1918), an eloquent if not necessarily persuasive diatribe enjoining the West to come to terms with Russia or else, "The Twelve " is not a piece of topical rhetoric. Nor is it a lyrical fugue such as that remarkable flight of historical imagination, " On the Kulikovo Field " (1908). It is rather a poetic *montage* where snatches of soldiers' songs, workers' ditties and the staccato rhythms of revolutionary marches are intertwined, only to merge toward the end into the stately chords of the baffling finale. It is an objective composition where the first-person pronoun appears only in the utterances of the protagonists such as Petka, the Red guardsman gone astray, but never as a vehicle of the author's self, where the distinctive voice of the poet is deliberately drowned in the cacophonous roar of the revolutionary street.

This is not to say that Blok was in fact morally neutral, toward the liberal intelligentsia opponents of the Bolshevik revolution. The " spiritual maximalist " had little use for what Briusov would have called half-measures. But this indubitable fact is more relevant to a frankly ideological ode such as " The Scythians " rather than " The Twelve." It is not Blok whose voice is heard in the deliberately coarse accents of the poem's opening section. It is the shrill discordant music of a city in turmoil that resounds in these pages. One could say that in " The Twelve," Blok, that profoundly personal if not narcissistic poet, curbed his need for self-expression to let the revolutionary chaos speak for itself. One might further argue that the structure of " The Twelve " was, in T. S. Eliot's much cited phrase, " the objective correlative " for that act of moral self-effacement, that refusal to exercise one's judgment vis-à-vis the "elements " which lay at the core of Blok's attitude in 1918. One may deplore, if one so chooses, the consequences and implications of such a refusal. But to label it a betrayal is both unfair and inaccurate since this unconditional surrender was thoroughly consistent with the pattern of Blok's fundamentally nonpolitical inward experiences to which he was referring in the above-quoted letter to his father.

Blok's note on " The Twelve," read in the wake of the poet's death at a commemorative session by his erstwhile friend and rival Andrei Belyi,[98] contains a revealing admission: " In January, 1918 [the month in which " The Twelve " was written] I gave myself to the elements for the last time as completely as I had in January, 1907 and in March, 1914." The above dates will mean little to the student of modern Russian history, but the biographer of Aleksandr Blok will have no trouble identifying them with Blok's two climactic romances. 1907 was the year of Blok's fateful encounter with the Petersburg actress Volokhova, the heroine of " The Snow Mask." In 1914 Blok was swept off his feet by L. A. Delmas, the " Carmen " of one of his finest lyrical sequences. The subject matter of " The Twelve " is thus shifted from the political to the erotic plane; where infatuation reigns supreme, where intellectual controls are swept away, with the poet overpowered once more by an irresistible passion the intellectual soundness of one's attitude becomes somewhat irrelevant. What matters is the Dionysian intoxication, the emotional intensity of being-in-love. Was the Revolution then another love object? In essence—yes. Some will remonstrate that most of the episodes in " The

[98] *Pamiati Aleksandra Bloka* [*To the Memory of Aleksandr Blok*] (Petersburg, 1922), p. 31.

Twelve " indicate an ambivalence toward, if not a revulsion from, the self-appointed apostles of the new order. But then which romance of the mature Blok was ever free from the love-hate duality, indeed, from intermittent awareness of, and a masochistic delight in, ego-shattering degradation?

Whatever the reader's or critic's ideological bias, it can scarcely be denied that this gratuitous act of total immersion in the music of the Revolution, of rapt listening to what Blok himself called "the noise produced by the crumbling of the old world," ushered in one of the memorable works of modern Russian poetry. Yet the price exacted by the poet's self-efface-ment seems to have been exorbitantly high.

According to reliable eyewitness testimony, Blok's passionate involvement with the revolutionary chaos was followed by an acute and ever-deepening depression. By 1919, a year after " The Twelve," he was suffering from utter exhaustion, weari-ness, and a growing sense of futility. His energy was sapped by an insidious and difficult to diagnose disease,[99] which lay wit-nesses were increasingly inclined to describe as a total atrophy of the will to live. (In his valuable monograph, K. Mochulskii cites a conversation which Blok had with a former Symbolist critic and scholar, G. Chulkov: "Would you like to die, Grigorii Ivanovitch?" asked Blok. Grigorii Ivanovitch an-swered either "No" or "I don't think so." Blok said, "And I want it very much.") [100]

Ever since Blok became a poet, he saw the creator's vocation, indeed his very *raison d'être* in his superior ability to hear and reproduce the "music of the world." In 1920 he thought this faculty of his eroded, or worse still, obsolete. His friend and admirer, Kornei Chukovskii reports in his memoir: "I kept asking him why he stopped writing poetry. He would answer invariably, 'All the sounds are dead. Don't you hear that there

[99] According to Mochulskii, several months before Blok's death his condition was diagnosed by experts as a combination of an endocrinitis with neurasthenia.
[100] Mochulskii, *Aleksandr Blok*, p. 439.

aren't any more sounds?'"[101]   Two years later Blok was dead. The curtain had fallen on the last act of a lyrical tragedy.

A somewhat doctrinaire and yet perceptive essay by Lev Trotsky written shortly after Blok's death contains a striking passage: "Of course, Blok was not ours, but he flung himself towards us. Having done so, he broke down."[102]

Whether Blok had flung himself toward Trotsky and Bolshevism as it actually was is open to question. It was the "permanent revolution" of his own utopian dreams, his personal vision of a "beautiful life" that Blok was pursuing in his headlong frenzy. In one crucial respect, however, Trotsky was right. This vulnerable, fragile lyrist broke down under the crushing burden of a superhuman moral strain. In doing so he lived up to the image of himself as a poet. His self-sacrifice was sincere and complete.

Briusov utilized his not inconsiderable resources and skills to become an influential and versatile man of letters. As a poet he seems today a representative rather than a major figure. Blok burned himself to ashes in serving the demon of music, but in the process produced some of the most haunting lyrics in the language. Should we conclude that in a poet the id is more essential than the ego, abandon more successful than control?

Not necessarily. For one thing, as any social scientist knows full well, drawing general inferences from a sample of two is a dubious procedure. For another, the undeniable if difficult-to-analyze fact of Blok's superior lyrical gifts makes a conclusion such as this less than meaningful. Moreover, while the importance to a lyrist of the relative availability of unconscious or preconscious materials cannot be gainsaid, in order to become poetry the emotional turmoil must be channeled and disciplined.

Blok's obsessive rhetoric should not be taken too literally.

---

[101] *Sovremenniki [Contemporaries]* (Moscow, 1962), p. 487.
[102] *Literatura i revoliutsiia* (Moscow, 1923), p. 90.

As a true Romantic, perhaps the last great Romantic in Russian poetry, he interpreted "music" not as an element of a verbal structure, but as its emotional matrix. Yet the reason why he was a major poet, in addition to being a complex and tragic literary figure, is that he found a poetic equivalent for the demon which possessed him, that he managed to transmute the music, to which he was listening so raptly, into verbal rhythms. Some of the keenest students of modern Russian poetry have pointed out that the chief source of that spellbinding effect which Blok's best verses so often achieve lies not in their imagery or in their euphony alone, but in their "magical" intonational pattern.[103] Few readers of "The Snow Mask," "In the Restaurant," "To the Muse," "On the Kulikovo Field," "Carmen," and many other lyrics or lyrical sequences of Blok's, will fail to see the point of this diagnosis whose documentation would require close textual analysis. All that needs to be emphasized here is that Blok could not have succeeded as a poet, had his Dionysian frenzy not been at once sustained and hemmed in by a formal principle, by aesthetic discipline. Blok was not unaware of this. In a letter written in 1912 he complained of the difficulties he encountered in his attempts to embrace a cause. Art, he averred, was the only realm where he felt at home: "I strive more and more towards strengthening artistic form since for me it is the only protection."[104] Both as man and as poet he needed all the protection poetic discipline could give him by keeping at bay the irrational chaos within, which threatened to overwhelm him, and by helping to turn it into verbal "music" that will endure.

---

[103] A brilliant Formalist critic Tynianov remarked parenthetically in his essay on Briusov: "Every time one thinks of Blok, one is reminded of some intonation which characterizes him alone." (*Arkhaisty i novatory* [Leningrad, 1929], p. 522).

[104] *Sud'ba Bloka*, ed. Nemerovskaia and Volpe, p. 172.

5. THE DEAD HAND OF THE FUTURE:

VLADIMIR MAIAKOVSKII

> *What meanness would you not commit, to*
> *Stamp our meanness?*
> *If, at last, you could change the world, what*
> *Would you think yourself too good for?*
> *Who are you?*
> *Sink into the mire*
> *Embrace the butcher, but*
> *Change the world: it needs it!*
> (Brecht, *Die Massnahme*)

In a recent memoir Iurii Olesha, one of the most sophisticated Soviet prose writers, recalls a conversation he once had with V. E. Meyerhold regarding a film version of Turgenev's *Fathers and Sons* which the famous *avant-garde* director was then contemplating. "I asked him whom he had in mind for the part of Bazarov. He answered: 'Maiakovskii.'"[1]

The resemblance between one of modern Russia's foremost poets and Turgenev's harshly antipoetic hero may not be immediately obvious. Yet a close look at Maiakovskii's poetry, especially at his earlier Futurist lyrics, reveals the presence of what might be called the Bazarov syndrome. The tenor of these Surrealist urban still-lives ("Night," "Morning," "The Street," etc.), these impassioned lyrical manifestoes ("I," "Man," "A Cloud in Trousers"), is total negation of the status quo.

"Glorify me," cried Maiakovskii in a poem written in 1914,

[1] Iurii Olesha, *Izbrannye sochineniia* [*Selected Works*] (Moscow, 1956), p. 46.

120

"For me the great are no match / Upon everything that has gone before / I stamp Nihil." Doubtless Maiakovskii's nihilism, not unlike Bazarov's, should not be confused with cynicism. It is rather a strident repudiation of all traditions, all authorities, all established standards (social, ethical, aesthetic), a personal commitment to a future, totally discontinuous with the "stifling past."

It is the savage intensity of this scorn, powerfully projected and strikingly phrased, that propelled Maiakovskii into the first ranks of prewar Russia's angry young men, the Futurists. It is the desperate urgency of his protest, magnified by a booming voice and a strikingly bold imagery, that made the twenty-year-old art student a recognized standard-bearer of the poetic *avant-garde* shortly after he had been discovered and hailed as a genius by that erratic yet shrewd impresario of the movement, David Burliuk.

Though the point has already been tellingly made by Roman Jakobson in his brilliant essay, "On the Generation Which Has Squandered Its Poets,"[2] it may be worth restating here: the mainsprings of Maiakovskii's revolt, as reflected in his pre-1917 lyrics and his most revealing Soviet poems, were not primarily political. His radicalism was that of a Bohemian rather than of a doctrinaire Marxist. This is not to deny such relevant facts as Maiakovskii's early involvement with the revolutionary movement, which cost him eleven months in prison when still a high-school boy or to question the sincerity of the retrospective statement in the poet's brief autobiography: "No work of art ever fascinated me more than Marx's 'Introduction'" [to the *Critique of Political Economy*]. Yet the image of the lone rebel which emerges from the violent, apocalyptic phraseology of his early works is more akin to François Villon or Verlaine, than it is to either Marx or Lenin. It is as *poète maudit*, a spokesman for, and a natural ally of, the metropolitan riffraff,

[2] *Smert' Vladimira Maiakovskogo* [*Death of Vladimir Maiakovski*] (Petropolis–Berlin, 1931).

" a twisted-lipped Zarathustra / of convicts of the city / lepro-
sarium " that the " I " confronts here the hostile crowd of solid
citizens:

But they [the outcasts] will not jeer at me, / they will not scorn
me. / They will strew my path with flowers like a prophet's / Every
damned one of these caved-in noses knows / I am your poet . . .
I alone will come through the buildings on fire / my body born
like a wafer by prostitutes / and held to heaven for their sins'
whitewashing.[3]

Several years later the main target of the poet's anger was to
be identified in political or topical terms, be it the " Entente "
(Left March) or world capitalism (" Hundred Fifty Million ").
But in his 1916 credo " Man," whose commanding images were
to reverberate through much of Maiakovskii's Soviet period,
the poet's chief "rival and foe" is that arch-enemy of the
modern artist—and we may add, of the Russian intelligentsia
—Philistinism. What is challenged here is not a definite social
order, but the very principle of order or stasis, everything that
smacks of tradition, of habit, or routine, everything that sets
limits to the creator's dishevelled, colossal sensibility. In a
word, a cluster, which an angry young Englishman is likely to
call the Establishment, but which in Russian literary usage is
covered by the virtually untranslatable word " *byt* " (the
closest approximations, depending on the context, are " circumstance," " mores," " everyday life," " daily grind "). The
quixotic one-man warfare against " *byt* " clearly could not be
won; hence the pessimism of the seldom-quoted passage from

[3]   Но меня не осудят, но меня не облают,
       как пророку, цветами устелят мне след.
       Все эти, провалившиеся носами, знают:
       я—ваш поэт.

       Как трактир, мне страшен ваш страшный суд!
       Меня одного сквозь горящие здания
       проститутки, как святыню, на руках понесут
       и покажут богу в свое оправдание.
              (V. Maiakovskii, *Sobranie stikhotvorenii* [Leningrad, 1950] II, 12.)

"Man" where the poet's inveterate foe, the epitome of smug respectability, is addressed thus: "Revolutions shake carcasses of kingdoms / The human herd changes its drivers. / But you, the uncrowned ruler of souls / no rebellion can unseat." [4]

The sense of battling against overwhelming odds is closely bound up here with the motif of an imminent defeat, of an impending doom. In "A Cloud in Trousers," "The Spine Flute," "Man," and in a short tragedy bearing the characteristic title "Vladimir Maiakovskii," the lyrical protagonist appears time and again as one born too early, a precursor and a martyr of a revolutionary Utopia, a St. John the Baptist of "the days to come," doomed to destruction at the hands of the invincible Philistines, or conversely the "last Mohican" of poetic sensibility:

I am bringing my soul on a plate / to the banquet of the ages to come. ("Vladimir Maiakovskii")

And I among you am its [the new age's] prophet. / I'm everywhere there's pain / In every living teardrop / I crucify myself again. ("A Cloud in Trousers")

Trickling down the unshaven cheek of a square / like a superfluous tear / I am / perhaps / the last poet. ("Vladimir Maiakovskii") [5]

The pervasive theme of martyrdom occasions here a wealth of religious imagery striking in a poet so militantly secular and so blatantly materialistic. Maiakovskii is keenly aware of this contradiction: "I who sing of machines and England / am perhaps no more than the thirteenth apostle / in the most

---

[4]   Встрясывают революции царств тельца,
        меняет погонщиков человечий табун,
        но тебя,
        некоронованного сердец владельца,
        ни один не трогает бунт!

                                                        (*Ibid.*, I, 171.)

[5]   . . . душу на блюде несу
        к обеду идущих лет.

                                                        (*Ibid.*, p. 65.)

ordinary gospel." [6]

The existential anguish which pervades these lines raises emotional frustration to the dignity of cosmic despair. In the savagely tender " A Cloud in Trousers," unrequited love becomes a paradigm of ultimate rejection and homelessness. (" I have no place to go.")

Was Maiakovskii's political commitment an attempt to escape the sense of moral alienation which he expressed so poignantly in his lyrical masterpiece? Or was he, on the eve of a major social upheaval, yielding to the temptations of political action and political power, yielding the more eagerly since Lenin's brutally decisive break with the old seemed to offer the closest equivalent to the Bohemian gospel of total negation and a shortcut to Utopia? Be that as it may, in November, 1917, Maiakovskii was ready to give his all to the Revolution, or, in his own words, " to offer all my sonorous powers of a poet to you, the attacking class."

Maiakovskii's verses, written in the first years of the revolution, breathe an almost physical exhilaration. In the city in turmoil, in the square, gripped by revolutionary excitement, he found an ideal resonator for his thundering voice, for his boisterous oratory. He felt at home amid the chaos and flux, when routine was displaced and " business as usual " discarded.

А я у вас—его предтеча;
Я—где боль, везде;
на каждой капле слёзовой течи
распял себя на кресте.

(*Ibid.*, p. 97.)

С небритой щеки площадей
стекая ненужной слезою,
Я,
Быть может,
последний поэт.

(*Ibid.*, p. 65.)

[6] Я, воспевающий машину и Англию,
может быть, просто,
в самом обыкновенном евангелии,
тринадцатый апостол.

(*Ibid.*, p. 102.)

Joyously Maiakovskii summoned into the street the Futurists, the "drummers" and the poets. He celebrated the "second tidal flood" in the powerful staccato of "Our March," a rare instance of fundamentally nonobjective poetry, where bursts of released consonantal energy provide an auditory correlative for a revolutionary euphoria. He sang the imminent world revolution in a satirical morality play "Mystery-Bouffe," and in a Communist epic "Hundred Fifty Million" (1920).

Interestingly enough, the party leaders were none too impressed. Lenin is known to have walked out on a vigorous rendition of Maiakovskii's "Our March." But then Lenin was avowedly a literary conservative who had little use for modern poetry. ("I prefer Pushkin," he said to a vociferous admirer of Maiakovskii.) The testimony of Lev Trotsky, whose literary sophistication was definitely superior to Lenin's, is of greater moment. In a perceptive, if somewhat priggish essay on futurism in *Literature and Revolution*, the Bolshevik statesman turned critic opined that "Maiakovskii's revolutionary individualism poured itself enthusiastically into the proletarian revolution, but did not blend with it."[7] Trotsky shrewdly noted in the very savagery of Maiakovskii ultramaterialistic attack on "the world-Romantic" accents of negative romanticism and expressed annoyance with the poet's "individualistic and Bohemian arrogance" which, ironically enough, was most apparent in the poem intended as an epic of mass heroism, "Hundred Fifty Million." The idea of portraying the final showdown between the revolutionary masses and world capitalism in the form of the hand-to-hand combat of Woodrow Wilson "swimming in fat" with a Russian superman, Ivan, bearing a distinct resemblance to Maiakovskii, struck Trotsky as extravagant and frivolous. Actually, one doesn't need to share Trotsky's impatience with that creative playfulness which to this reader is the most attractive, indeed the redeem-

[7] Lev Trotsky, *Literature and Revolution* (New York, 1925), p. 149.

ing feature of "Hundred Fifty Million," to concur in his basic diagnosis: Maiakovskii's strenuous attempt to submerge in the collective will his elephantine ego ("no one is the author of this poem of mine") resulted in another act of self-dramatization. "Our poet," says Trotsky aptly, "is a Maiakomorphist: When he wants to elevate man he makes him be Maiakovskii."[8]

This persistent urge towards self-aggrandizement was curiously intertwined with self-denial and self-denigration, with a frenzied effort to demean poetic craft to the level of a mere handmaiden of journalism. Thus while Trotsky was chiding Maiakovskii for his Bohemian arrogance, A. V. Lunacharskii, the first Soviet commissar of education and Maiakovskii's most influential protector, was gently taking the poet to task for his excessively "humble" or humdrum notion of poetry. Lunacharskii was mildly shocked by Maiakovskii's insistence that "today the poet's chief task is to complain in brisk verse about the bad pavements on Miasnitskaia street" (a street in Moscow).[9] The traditional roles are reversed here with the cultural bureaucrat upholding the dignity and glamour of the poet's calling, while the poet strenuously urges a narrowly topical and utilitarian view of his job.

This curious polemic epitomizes an important facet of Maiakovskii's political commitment: no propagandistic chore was too menial for him. He wrote marches and versified slogans and Soviet commercials; he produced thousands of posters and captions deriding the opponents of the regime and eulogizing the Soviet institutions, including the dread Cheka. In his moving farewell poem, "At the Top of My Voice" (1930), written on the eve of his suicide, he spoke of himself as a "latrine cleaner and water carrier / by the revolution / mobilized and called to colors / who went off to the front / from the

---

[8] *Ibid.*, p. 150.
[9] Cf., V. Katanian, *Maiakovskii, Literaturnaia khronika* [*Maiakovskii, Literary Chronicle*] (Leningrad, 1948).

aristocratic garden / of poetry / the capricious wench." [10] He debunked any poetry which wasn't immediately useful: "In our days only he is a poet who will write a march and a slogan." Indeed, sometimes—as Gleb Struve has recently reminded us [11] —he would go as far as to deny being a poet: "They say Maiakovskii, don't you see, is a poet, so let him sit on his poetic bench. I do not give a hoot about being a poet. I am not a poet, but first of all a man who put his pen at the service—at the service, mind you—of the present moment, of today's reality and its standard-bearer, the Soviet government and the Party." This eagerness to serve would occasion such passages as the embarrassing plea for party control over poetry found in a 1925 poem:

I want . . . / the Gosplan [State Economic Planning Commission] / to sweat / in debate / assigning me / goals a year ahead. / I want the factory committee / to lock / my lips / when the work is done / I want / the pen to be on a par with the bayonet / and Stalin / to deliver his Politbiuro / reports about verse in the making / as he would about pig iron and the smelting of steel.[12]

---

[10] Я, ассенизатор
                       и водовоз,
        революцией
                     мобилизованный и призванный,
        ушел на фронт
                     из барских садоводств
        поэзии—
                  бабы капризной.
                                     (Maiakovskii, *Sobranie stikhotvorenii*, I, 579.)

[11] *Novyi Zhurnal [New Review]*, XLVIII (March, 1957), 260–61.

[12] Я хочу,
           чтоб в дебатах
                        потел Госплан,
        Мне давая
              задания на год.

        .   .   .   .

        Я хочу,
            чтоб в конце работы
                     завком

It isn't easy to disentangle all the implications of the above. Was Maiakovskii affirming the importance of poetry in the only language which Russia's iron age could understand—in that of technology and political expediency? Was this another expression of the Futurist innovator's urge to depoeticize poetry, to eschew the hieratic solemnity of the Symbolist pundit and the sweet mellifluousness of traditional lyrics for the sake of a harsher and more vigorous poetic fare? Perhaps. And yet the spectacle of the impudent rebel begging the Party for directives is a profoundly disturbing one. The total loyalty to a political blueprint of the future verges here on aesthetic masochism.[13]

It would not be historically accurate to blame this frenzied "conformism" on external pressures alone. That during the last years of his life Maiakovskii was often harassed by envious hacks and zealots is a matter of record. But his act, to use his own words, "of stepping on the throat of my song" for the greater glory of the cause was largely a voluntary, spontaneous gesture. It is interesting to note in this connection that the slogan of "social command" which during the last thirty

---

запирал мои губы.
        замком.
Я хочу,
      чтоб к штыку
           приравняли перо.
С чугуном чтоб.
         и с выделкой стали
о работе стихов,
        от Политбюро,
чтобы делал
      доклады Сталин.

(Maiakovskii, *Sobranie stikhotvorenii*, II, 336.)

[13] In a retrospective poem "Maiakovskii Begins" 1936–39) one of the most gifted neo-Futurist poets, N. Aseev, recalls a curious conversation he once had with Maiakovskii. What would you do, Maiakovskii asked Aseev, if "they" were to issue a decree that from now on everybody had to write in iambic meter. Taken aback by this strange query, Aseev finally averred that he did not think he could do this. Maiakovskii fell silent for a while and glumly declared: "And I *would* write in iambs." (N. Aseev, *Izbrannoe* [*Selected Poems*] Moscow, 1948.)

years has come to epitomize bureaucratic dictation to the writer had been proclaimed in the early twenties by the neo-Futurist group *Lef* (Left Front) of which Maiakovskii was one of the leading members. This short-lived and strident faction sought to combine *avant-garde* experimentation with blatant political instrumentalism. There is considerable irony in the fact that the tenet which became a club in the hands of the Socialist-Realist hacks was first introduced by a group of wayward innovators to whom " social command " meant a spontaneous response of the poet to the " body and pressure of time."

Did Maiakovskii's eagerness to subordinate his work to extra-poetic demands and criteria lead to a debasement of his art and a corrosion of his creative powers? Boris Pasternak seems to imply as much when in *I Remember* he speaks of Maiakovskii's political verse as " clumsily-rhymed sermons, cultivated insipidity, those commonplaces and platitudes set forth so artificially, so confusedly and so devoid of humor." [14]

Many will find this too harsh and too blanket an indictment. The qualities which characterized the early Maiakovskii—verbal inventiveness, coarse but vigorous wit, delight in, and uncanny adeptness at, striking, unorthodox rhymes—are present in varying degrees in his Soviet productions and make many a jingle of Maiakovskii's a more vital work of poetry than the most ambitious poems of dutifully proletarian versifiers. In fact, when viewed against the background of the Kazins, the Zharovs, the Bezymenskiis, Maiakovskii looms up like a giant among pygmies; or should one rather say, a crippled giant?

For when all is said and done, there is precious little in Maiakovskii's bulky post-1917 output to rival the striking power and the imaginative freshness of " A Cloud in Trousers." Eloquent passages in Maiakovskii's two programmatic poems, " V. I. Lenin " and " Well Done!," the deftly ingenious rhymes of some of his occasional verse, the vitality and gusto of several

[14] B. Pasternak, " Avtobiograficheskii ocherk," *Sochineniia,* II, 43.

American poems (e. g., "The Brooklyn Bridge"), celebrating the encounter of a Futurist imagination with U. S. technology (Maiakovskii visited the United States in 1925), none of this can quite compensate for the reams of journalistic bombast, of strenuous Red-flag waving, not devoid of rhetorical effectiveness, but unworthy of Maiakovskii.

It is probably no accident that this poetic champion of Bolshevism is most genuinely and effectively himself in his nonconformist or nonpolitical works. Maiakovskii's plays, "The Bedbug" (1928) and "The Bathhouse" (1929), eloquently attest to his gift for savage satire, sharpened by his growing dismay at the rise of Soviet neo-Philistinism. In "About This" (1923) or "A letter from Paris to Comrade Kostrov on the Nature of Love" (1928), the pent-up lyrical urge, bursting the fetters of self-imposed restraint and of civic taboos, "sweeps everything else aside" ("About This") to proclaim the untractable, uncontrollable, elemental power of personal emotions.

Clearly, Maiakovskii's bondage to the future was taking a heavy toll from the poet and the man alike. By the middle of the twenties the ebullience of "Our March" had given way to somber stoicism tinged with weariness. In 1925 the future suicide was chiding his fellow poet, the wayward peasant lyrist, Sergei Esenin, who had just hanged himself in a Leningrad hotel, for having taken an easy way out: "In this life it isn't difficult to die, to build life is much more difficult." The main advantage of life seems now to lie in its being the harder course of action. Two years later, in one of the most spirited poems of that period, "A Conversation with a Tax Collector about Poetry," Maiakovskii was confessing: "There is less and less love / there is less and less daring / and time / is a battering ram / against my head / then comes the deadliest of all amortizations / the amortization of the heart and soul." [15] In 1928 Maiakovskii was engaged in writing a poem "Badly

---

[15]   Все меньше любится

.все меньше дерзается

Done!," clearly a polemic with his own earlier epic of the October revolution, "Well Done!" He was telling his friends that only a good, great love could save him from what was apparently a growing depression and disillusionment.

The great love came promptly, indeed in Maiakovskii's own words, burst upon the scene like a "hurricane." But instead of providing a way out, the new emotional involvement proved to be a trap. During a visit in Paris in 1928 Maiakovskii fell in love with a young Russian *émigré*, Tatiana Iakovleva. A year later, having failed to persuade Tatiana to return to Russia, Maiakovskii applied for another visa to Paris. The request was denied; apparently the authorities did not fully trust the Soviet patriotism of a man who shortly after his death was to be proclaimed by no less a figure than Stalin as "the best and most talented poet of the Soviet epoch."

In April, 1930, Maiakovskii shot himself through the heart leaving behind the much quoted suicide note. Its key lines are chilling in their uncanny casualness, in their thoroughly un-maiakovskian restraint: "as they say, the incident is closed. / Love boat has smashed against circumstance." In the original the last word is characteristically "*byt*," Maiakovskii's chief term of opprobrium. The stolid, ordinary "reality" has caught up with Maiakovskii and defeated him, as back in 1916 he said it would. But this time the dull force which crushed the poet's "great love," was to a large extent a matter of artificial barriers erected by the very regime which Maiakovskii had embraced as a major ally in his losing battle against the deadly pull of routine.

Was it ideological disenchantment or emotional frustration

и лоб мой
        время
                с разбега крушит.
Приходит
           страшнейшая из амортизаций—
амортизация
               сердца и души.

(Maiakovskii, II, 347–48.)

that triggered off the catastrophe? The matter is too complex to permit of a single explanation. Clearly, the ultimate causes of Maiakovskii's self-destructive act lie deeper than that. Both the *émigré* publicists who saw in Maiakovskii simply another victim of Communist dictatorship and the dutiful Soviet hacks mumbling sheepishly about a sudden and totally unexpected loss of nerve were properly reminded by Roman Jakobson[16] that the theme of the poet's suicide, of gambling one's life away, had haunted Maiakovskii's poetry ever since 1915. The death wish, the tragic crack (*nadryv*), the Kirilov- or Bazarov-like loneliness had been there from the beginning. The "engagement" had not eliminated these attitudes. It had merely driven them underground. In the last years of the poet's life the despair which howled in his Futurist lyrics seems to have reasserted itself with a redoubled force.

The millennium so eagerly anticipated, so ardently sought, eluded the poet's grasp. Bolshevism let Maiakovskii down; but so in all fairness would have any political system, any stabilized mode of societal existence. More importantly, voluntary sacrifices made en route to the ever-receding Utopia proved costly and self-defeating. The grim single-mindedness of the Bolshevik creed, espoused with an *outré* Bohemian frenzy, encouraged lyrical suicide and thus threatened the very qualities affirmed in the initial act of total defiance—untrammeled self-expression, emotional spontaneity.

Herein lies the tragic dialectics of Maiakovskii's predicament: it is primarily as an embattled artist that he refused the entrance ticket to the world he never made. Yet in his headlong rush toward a future worthy of a poet, he had propelled himself into a situation which rendered all genuine poetry impossible. One is reminded of that archetypal *poète maudit*, Arthur Rimbaud, who, in recoiling from the stifling Philistinism of the French provincial *bourgeoisie*, ran all the way, only to land at the trading posts of an Africa, where the poet's voice was wholly lost.

[16] Pasternak, *Smert' Vladimira Maiakovskogo*.

6. "LIFE BY VERSES": BORIS PASTERNAK

" Leave to the poets their moments of joy
Lest your world perish."   (Miłosz)

1.

In his brilliant spiritual autobiography *Safe Conduct*, as well
as in his more recent autobiographical sketch,[1] Pasternak looks
back reflectively on the forces which helped to shape the style
of his early writings. He speaks of his profound affinity, and
admiration as a budding poet, for Vladimir Maiakovskii and
of his equally strong urge to evolve a distinctive poetic manner.
" So as not to echo him [Maiakovskii] . . . and not to be taken
for his imitator, I proceeded to get rid of the heroic tone, which
in my case would have been false, and of any straining for
effect."[2]   Elsewhere he put it thus: " I abandoned the Romantic manner. And that is how the non-Romantic style of *Above
the Barriers*[3] came about."[4]   He further suggests that this
abandonment of the Romantic manner entailed a break with

[1] Boris Pasternak, " Avtobiograficheskii ocherk " [An Autobiographical Sketch],
Sochineniia [*Works*] (Ann Arbor, 1961), II, 1–52.
[2] *Ibid.*, p. 41.
[3] Pasternak's first important collection of verses. The poems included in it were
written between 1914 and 1916.
[4] " Safe Conduct," quoted from *Boris Pasternak, Selected Writings* (New York,
1949), p. 128.

the " whole conception of life " which underlies it, more specifically, with the Romantic image of the poet. This image Pasternak described in a telling phrase as " the notion of biography
as spectacle." [5]

Few students of modern literature will fail to appreciate the
import of this formula. As I have been trying to suggest
above,[6] the two interlocking attitudes which it highlights—the
poet's tendency to dramatize himself in his work, and conversely to turn his life into lyrical drama—loom very large
indeed in the early twentieth-century Russian poetry.

In Russian symbolism the boundary between life and art
was perilously fluid. The poet's work served all too often to
project the *fin-de-siècle* myth of the artist as a seer, a rebel, or
both; the poet's biography—to bear witness to that myth. In
this respect, as in some others, the Futurist iconoclast, Maiakovskii, was much closer to the Symbolist tradition than he
knew or was ever prepared to admit. The " notion of biography
as spectacle " is no less relevant to the life and work of Sergei
Esenin. His confessional verses which time and again verge on
lyrical exhibitionism were above all a vehicle for dramatizing
the author's personal plight—that of a nostalgic and wayward
peasant poet, " the last village bard," crushed by the inexorable
demands of the iron age.[7] Like Blok, both Maiakovskii and
Esenin were regarded by their public primarily as literary
figures, embodied poetic destinies, rather than as mere poets,
i. e., creators of poetic values.

To at least one British critic the poetry of Boris Pasternak,

[5] Mr. Robert Payne, the translator of *Safe Conduct*, renders the above as the
" scenic conception of biography " (*Ibid.*, p. 129). I find the " notion of biography
as spectacle " a more intelligible equivalent.

[6] See above, " The Maker and the Seer," " The Dead Hand of the Future."

[7] In a brief autobiographical sketch, reprinted in a recent selection from Esenin's
poetry (*Sergei Esenin* [Moscow, 1958], pp. 3–5), after a recital of some basic in-
formation, Esenin says: " As for additional autobiographical data, they can be
found in my poems." To be sure this statement is not to be taken literally. No body
of poetry, however " confessional," can be treated as documentary evidence. Yet
whether or not Esenin's work always reflects accurately his actual experience is not
at issue here. The point is that it purports to do so.

seen against the background of "the agonies and perorations of Esenin and Maiakovskii," appears as nearly devoid of biographical traits: "a Parthenon of impersonality," writes George Reavey, in "A First Essay toward Pasternak."[8] Reavey's assertion may seem to many of us highly questionable. The recent specious official charges of Pasternak's "narcissistic self-centredness" or "individualistic subjectivism" can safely be disregarded. But how about Pasternak's own reference to the "fragmentary, personal" nature of his first writings?[9] How about the lyrical excitement which pervades so many of Pasternak's poetic cycles, especially his incomparably vital *My Sister, Life* (1921), and the uniquely personal, idiosyncratic quality of the Pasternakian vision?

Clearly, the matter is highly complex, if not elusive. The poetry of Pasternak—introspective, but not self-oriented, deeply lyrical and yet more than personal, a poetry which combines the emotional intensity of a Dylan Thomas with an uncanny sharpness of sensory detail—plays havoc with hard-and-fast distinctions and discourages rigid dichotomies. But while it would be futile and presumptuous to try to resolve the apparent paradox of Pasternak's poetic craft, an attempt to redefine the problem might be useful and worth while. This calls for a somewhat closer look at the implicit as well as the explicit notions which Pasternak has of poetry and at the status of "the self" in the unique poetic world which bears his signature.

In a recent essay, Renato Poggioli makes an important observation: "The raw material of Pasternak's poetry is introspection. Yet Pasternak treats the self as object rather than as subject. Thus, in a nonmystical sense one could apply to him Rimbaud's formula: '*car je suis un autre.*'"[10] This brings out

---

[8] *Experiment*, No. 6 (1930), pp. 14–17.

[9] From a recent letter to a Uruguayan magazine editor, quoted by N. Chiaromonte in "Pasternak's Message," *Partisan Review* (Winter, 1958), pp. 127–34.

[10] "Boris Pasternak," *Partisan Review* (Fall, 1958).

an essential aspect of the Pasternakian manner—the virtual absence of the lyrical "hero." The "I" in Pasternak's poetry, or artistic prose for that matter, is not the pivot of a lyrical narrative, the principal point of reference. The self exists here, as it were, on a par with all other elements of this heterogeneous universe—natural phenomena, inanimate objects, indeed with its own objectified sensations and states of mind. An integral part of his physical environment, of nature, he is treated as "object" also in that he is no more likely to act than to be acted upon, looked at, appraised by, the things around him. This is how the remarkable poem "Marburg" (1916) describes its "hero" in a state of emotional shock: "I went out into the square. I could have been considered born anew. Each trifle lived and, setting little store by me, rose in its final significance."[11] In a much later "Ballad" we find the following lines: "I wake up. I am encompassed by the discovered. / I am taken stock of."[12] Indeed we might be tempted to say that the self is reduced here to the passive status of a mere thing if it were not for the apparent humanization of nature itself. The world of objects and natural phenomena to which the image of the author is assimilated throbs with lyrical dynamism, glows with an all-pervading emotion.

In an important theoretical passage in *Safe Conduct*, Pasternak says somewhat cryptically: "Focused on a reality which feeling has displaced, art is a record of this displacement."[13] Clearly, the two key terms here are "displacement" and "feeling." The former seems to point towards that ultramodern

---

[11]   Я вышел на площадь. Я мог быть сочтен
         Вторично родившимся. Каждая малость
         Жила и, не ставя меня ни во что,
         В прощальном значеньи своем подымалась.

                                        (Boris Pasternak, *Sochineniia*, I, 220.)

[12]   Я просыпаюсь. Я объят
         Открывшимся. Я на учете.

                                                    (*Ibid.*, p. 331.)

[13] Boris Pasternak, *Selected Writings*, p. 72.

quality of Pasternak's poetic art which could be described with Viktor Shklovskii as " semantic shift," and with Ezra Pound as a tendency towards the " unification of disparate ideas." Pasternak's bold, startling imagery reshuffles ordinary relationships and hierarchies by juxtaposing the most divergent notions and spheres of experience, by holding together within the compass of one stanza " seas stirred by breezes from Morocco, the simoon, . . . Archangel snoring in snows, . . . dawn on the Ganges," and the drying of a manuscript of Pushkin's " The Prophet." [14]

It is feeling, Pasternak reminds us, which serves here as a reorganizing, displacing and yet integrating power. What kind of feeling is it? And how does the integration occur? Elsewhere, in a poem " Definition of Creativity," [15] this power is identified as " passion."

> Gardens, ponds and palings, the creation
> Foam-flecked with the whiteness of our weeping,
> Are nothing but categories of passion
> That the human heart has had in keeping.[16]

As Sir Isaiah Berlin has already pointed out,[17] it would be to misjudge the nature and the uses of this passion to consider these lines as merely another instance of the pathetic fallacy. For one thing, nature in Pasternak is not a screen on to which to project the author's personal feelings and moods. More broadly, it is not the Baudelairian *" forêt des symboles "* nor a

---

[14] Pasternak, *Sochineniia*, I, 67; the English translation appears in *Boris Pasternak, Selected Writings*, pp. 266–67, and, more recently, in *Poems* by Boris Pasternak, translated by L. Slater (London, 1958).

[15] Pasternak, *Selected Writings*, p. 33.

[16] Quoted from, Maurice Bowra, *The Creative Experiment* (London, 1949).

> И сады, и пруды, и ограды,
> И кипящее белыми воплями
> Мирозданье—лишь страсти разряды,
> Человеческим сердцем накопленной.

(Sochineniia, I, 24.)

[17] " The Energy of Pasternak," *Partisan Review* (1950), pp. 748–51.

set of T. S. Eliot's "objective correlatives" for specific human emotions.[18] In Blok's poetry, the recurrent image of the snow-storm is typically a symbol of an emotional turmoil or a social cataclysm. Pasternak's favorite motif, that of a "shower," a "downpour," has a different status. The rain appears here as an elemental force. Its attractiveness to the poet may lie in its association with freshness, movement, transformation, renewal. But all these dynamic qualities or events are apprehended as part of nature. The image does not point beyond itself, does not serve as a proxy for any recognizable human situation. In "After a Rain," "My Sister, Life" and many other rain-soaked poems of Pasternak, the shower is a source of delight, the focus of lyrical excitement, but not its emblem.

More important, perhaps, the feeling which informs Paster-nak's poems is not the stuff of which most lyrical narratives are made. This is not to minimize the importance of the erotic motif in Pasternak's work (some of his finest poems are love lyrics), or to ignore the personal genesis of lyrical cycles such as "Separation" in *Themes and Variations* (1923). Yet, when all is said and done, it is not the love of Boris Pasternak for another human being which provides the central theme and the integrating principle in this discordant welter of images, objects, and sensations. It is something much less tangible or personal —something akin to cosmic ecstasy, to an "oceanic feeling," as a Freudian would put it, or, in Sir Isaiah Berlin's words, to "a metaphysical emotion which melts the barrier between personal experience and brute creation."[19] To put it rather differently, what is projected here is not a particular emotion but emotion-ality as a faculty of the human heart, as a generic form of the human psyche.[20] What is celebrated is not a specific affective

---

[18] T. S. Eliot, *Selected Essays* (London, 1951).

[19] Berlin, "The Energy of Pasternak."

[20] It may not be too farfetched to see in this world-view, which implies that "objective reality" is organized by an "intersubjective" principle, a poetic extension of neo-Kantianism. Perhaps Pasternak's brief apprenticeship with Professor Cohen of Marburg has not been in vain.

experience, but the very process of experiencing, the joy and the thrill of feeling, sensing, responding, of rubbing shoulders with "my sister, life." (What other poet would have thought of calling life his sister?)

This joy of existence is primordial, and is so fundamental an aspect of Pasternak's *Weltgefühl* as to be literally irrepressible, undaunted. Asserting itself time and again, as T. S. Eliot would phrase it, "in excess of facts as they appear,"[21] the Pasternakian ecstasy fills his more buoyant poems to the brim (in "Our Storm" the poet asks almost helplessly: "What shall I do with my joy?"),[22] and proves nearly impervious to disappointment and defeat. "How can there be melancholy when there is so much joy?" he asks in *Safe Conduct*. The early poem "Marburg," already quoted, is ostensibly about a major emotional setback: the poet proposes to his beloved and is turned down; from a characteristically vague passage in *Safe Conduct* it can be inferred that the poem echoes an actual occurrence. Yet not even the hero's anguish can silence the incongruous note of bliss.[23] In Iurii Zhivago's solitary meditations about the nature of art this attitude to life is formulated and made an aesthetic canon: " ... Every work of art, including tragedy, witnesses to the joy of existence." Pasternak seems to have espoused and actually voiced this notion even before he became a "practicing" poet. In his recent autobiographical sketch he restates the principal theses of a lecture entitled "Symbolism and Immortality" which he delivered in Moscow in 1910. He argued then that art is primarily concerned with the transcendent, supra-personal aspect of "generic human subjectivity." He also said that "though an artist is naturally a mortal like everyone of us, the joy of existence[24] which he

[21] Eliot, *Selected Essays*.

[22] Pasternak, *Stikhotvoreniia*, p. 35.

[23] A deliberately ambiguous line, "ia sviatogo blazhennei" hovers between "I am more *blissful* than a saint" and "I am more *blessed* than a saint."

[24] Boris Pasternak, *Doctor Zhivago*, trans. Max Hayward and Manya Harari (London, 1958), p. 407.

experienced was immortal . . . Owing to his works, others will be able to experience it . . . , a hundred years later, in a kind of adherence to the personal and intimate form of his first sensations." [25]

We may note, along with the linking of art with the joy of existence, which is the *idée maîtresse* of Pasternak's aesthetics, the further motif of self-transcendence. This is equally apparent in Pasternak's view of the creative process as reflected in *Doctor Zhivago*:

> After two or three stanzas and several images by which he was himself astonished, his work took possession of him and he experienced the approach of what is called inspiration. At such moments . . . the ascendancy is no longer with the artist or the state of mind which he is trying to express, but with language, his instrument of expression. Language, the home and dwelling of beauty and meaning, itself begins to think and speak for man and turns wholly to music. . . .
>
> At such moments Iurii felt that the main part of his work was not being done by him but by something which was above him and controlling him: the thought and poetry of the world as it was at that moment and as it would be in the future.[26]

This passage does not necessarily imply a mystical notion of the creative act. It rather suggests a poetics which pays less heed to the poet and his personality than to the internal laws and exigencies of poetic language.

The connection between these tenets and the impersonal or nonsubjective tenor of much of Pasternak's poetry is apparent enough. His work does not so much project a coherent and dramatically effective image of the poet as dramatize what Edgar Allan Poe calls the poetic principle—the power which brings the poem into being. Is not that joy of heightened perception, of passionate seeing, which provides the emotional leitmotiv of Pasternak's poetry, the essential quality and the unique prerogative of creative imagination? No wonder that

[25] *Ibid.*, pp. 25–26.   [26] *Ibid.*, pp. 391–92.

Pasternak's most characteristic collection of verse *My Sister, Life* contains so many, and highly unorthodox, attempts to define poetry and the creative process. In "Definition of Poetry" poetic creation is defined without any reference to the creator in a series of striking images, disparate but held together by some inner euphonic and emotional vibration: [27]

> It's a whistle's precipitous rise,
> It is icicles broken and ringing,
> It is night when the frost on leaves lies,
> It's a duel of nightingales singing.[28]

Perhaps even more revealing is "Poetry" where Pasternak says rather unexpectedly: "You are a summer with a third-class ticket / You are a suburb, not a refrain." [29] One might be tempted to dismiss this as the most bizarre or whimsical " defence of poesie " yet offered. But the import of these lines is not as cryptic as it appears. Poetry, Pasternak seems to suggest, is not a soft musical background for, or a verbal accompaniment to, the life of action; it is the things themselves, the most prosaic, humdrum everyday objects or occurrences, rediscovered, displaced, transfigured. It is the world become language.

---

[27] " In art," Pasternak says in *Safe Conduct,* " the man is silent and only the image speaks."

[28] Quoted from Maurice Bowra, *The Creative Experiment,* London, 1949.

> Это—круто налившийся свист.
> Это—щелканье сдавленных льдинок.
> Это—ночь, леденящая лист.
> Это—двух соловьев поединок.

(Sochineniia, I, 22.)

[29]
> Ты—лето с местом в третьем классе,
> Ты—пригород, а не припев.

(Sochineniia, I, 101.)

2.

It was this immersion in the creative interplay between words and things, this intoxication with verbal magic, which made Pasternak, in a poem dated 1917, look out from his attic still dazed from an encounter with Byron and Edgar Allan Poe, and call to the children playing in the yard below: "What millennium is there outside, dears?" [30] It was likewise a quiet dedication to the unheroic yet exacting task of rendering his vision with the utmost accuracy, a dedication coupled with his congenital reticence and shyness, which induced him to persist in shunning the "notion of biography as spectacle." He expressed this more recently in somewhat more personal terms: "A life without secrets and without privacy, a life brilliantly reflected in the mirror of a show window is inconceivable for me." [31]

Here for once was a master of the modern Russian poetic idiom who refused to serve as a banner or a symbol, who did not want to stylize his life into a Passion play spectacularly testifying to a larger truth or dramatically challenging the Philistines. Here for once was a poet who spurned the romantic temptations of prophecy and proposed to attend to his own business—the engrossing minutiae of the poetic craft.

But the events which followed the appearance of his *Doctor Zhivago* in translation abroad, when its publication in his own country was not allowed, abruptly propelled Pasternak into the very limelight which he had studiously sought to avoid and made his name an epitome and a symbol for many people all over the world who had never seen a single example of his work: the epitome of the inwardly free poet in an unfree society, the symbol of embattled creative integrity.

[30] *Ibid.*, p. 4.
[31] Pasternak, *Sochineniia*, II, 44.

This does not necessarily mean that Pasternak had felt compelled to abandon his initial commitment to noncommitment,
his unspectacular notion of biography. Paradoxically, it is
precisely Pasternak's insistence on preserving his emotional and
poetic privacy that has now made him a public figure. In
choosing a life of contemplation and creativity, Pasternak followed his true nature or that of his poetic gift. But he reckoned without the nature of the age whose heavy shadow fell
across his path.

Not that Pasternak has ever tried to insulate himself against
the " body and pressure of time." His sense of history should
not be judged solely or even primarily by the absent-minded
question in his 1917 poem. Keeping his fine sensibility available
to historical experience, he did not fail to respond to the elemental sweep of the Revolution, now with bewilderment, now
with sympathetic fascination. As Marina Tsvetaeva put it: in
the summer of 1917 " he walked alongside the revolution and
listened to it raptly." [32] He tried to absorb and accept the new
realities, but on his own terms and at his own pace: that is, as
an uncommitted poet rather than as a shrill propagandist. His
interesting, though not altogether successful, epic fragments,
" Year 1905 " and " Lieutenant Schmidt," represent an honest
effort to grasp the meaning of the Revolution by recreating
its antecedents. Yet he would not be used or rushed. " In an
epoch of tempo," he once said, " one ought to think slowly."
He would not be dragooned into " well-intentioned " (i. e.,
politically orthodox) platitudes: " Hell is paved with good
intentions. A view has prevailed, that if one paves verses with
them all is forgiven." [33]

---

[32] Marina Tsvetaeva, " Svetovoi liven' " [Luminous Downpour] in *Proza* (New
York, 1956).

[33]   Благими намереньями вымощен ад.
        Установился взгляд,,
        Что, если вымостить ими стихи,
        Простятся все грехи.
                (" Vysokaia bolezn' " [Lofty Disease], *Sochineniia*, I, 264.)

Characteristically it was not until the early thirties when Russian literature was whipped into conformity that the sense of grim foreboding entered the life-affirming poetry of Pasternak. At first, the note was sounded with Pasternak's characteristic cryptic reticence:

> It's vain in days when the great Soviet convenes,
> When highest passion runs in flooding tide,
> To seek a place for poets on the scene,
> It's dangerous, if not unoccupied.[34]

But it became clearer in the following poem of 1932:

> If only, when I made my debut,
> There might have been a way to tell
> That lines with blood in them can murder,
> That they can flood the throat and kill.
>
> I certainly would have rejected
> A jest on such a sour note,
> So bashful was that early interest,
> The start was something so remote.
>
> But age is pagan Rome, demanding
> No balderdash, no measured breath,
> No fine feigned parody of dying,
> But really being done to death.
>
> A line that feeling sternly dictates
> Sends on the stage a slave and that

---

[34] The translation is Mr. S. Schimanski's (Boris Pasternak, *The Collected Prose Works* [London, 1945], p. 37). But I have allowed myself to substitute "the great Soviet convenes" for "councils great convene."

Напрасно в дни великого совета,
Где высшей страсти отданы места,
Оставлена вакансия поэта:
Она опасна, если не пуста.

(*Sochineniia*, I, 223.)

Means that the task of art is ended
And there's a breath of earth and fate.[35]

" A breath of earth and fate." The obtrusive theme of modern
Russian poetry—that of the poet's tragic destiny—had finally
caught up with Boris Pasternak. Apparently, " life by verses " [36]
was proving increasingly incompatible with the kind of commitment and the style of life fostered by the Russian society
of the 1930's.

When culture is treated as a weapon and literature as a
source of moral edification, poetic detachment smacks of sabo-
tage. When politics is viewed as the highest form of human
activity, aesthetic contemplation seems an act of political defiance. When the dry-as-dust abstractions of an official ide-

---

[35] The translation is by Babette Deutsch, with the exception of the last stanza
which is drawn from Sir Maurice Bowra's version (see Pasternak, *Selected Writings*).

О, знал бы я, что так бывает,
Когда пускался на дебют,
Что строчки с кровью—убивают,
Нахлынут горлом и убьют!

От шуток с этой подоплекой
Я б отказался наотрез.
Начало было так далеко,
Так робок первый интерес.

Но старость—это Рим, который
Взамен турусов и колес
Не читки требует с актера,
А полной гибели всерьез.

Когка строку диктует чувство,
Оно на сцену шлет раба,
И тут кончается искусство,
И дышат почва и судьба.   (*Sochineniia*, I, 351.)

The same device of thinly disguising the face of the poet under the mask of an
actor is employed in one of the most effective poems in the Zhivago cycle entitled
" Hamlet." It is ironical that the *motif* of the stage—and the theme of a dan-
gerous symbiosis of the actor's part with his life— should increasingly intrude upon
the work of one who, at the outset of his career, explicitly disowned the " stagy "
notion of poetic biography.

[36] " Thus one begins to live by verses," ends a memorable poem from " Themes
and Variations," *Sochineniia*, I, 85.

ology are increasingly used to displace reality and explain it away, even such politically innocuous qualities as delight in the sensory texture of things and worship of "the omnipotent god of details" [37] are likely to appear as utter irrelevance and escapism.

This irreconcilable conflict between the outlook of the poet and the party activist lies at the core of *Doctor Zhivago* which is not merely Pasternak's first full-length work of fiction, but his first successful attempt to reach beyond the realm of lyrical emotion—of what he himself has called the "personal and fragmentary"—towards the fundamental moral dilemmas of our time. It is perhaps the crowning paradox of his paradox-ridden career that this one epic of his should be in a sense more personal and autobiographical than many of his lyrics. In spite of its panoramic scope and wide moral relevance, *Doctor Zhivago* is above all the poetic biography of a richly endowed individual and the story of his unremitting efforts to maintain his creative integrity amid the overwhelming pressures of an age of wars and revolutions. True, Iurii Andreevich Zhivago cannot wholly be identified with Boris Pasternak: to confuse a literary character with its creator is always a dubious procedure. But the kinship between the two is not easily overestimated; and it is nowhere more apparent than in Zhivago's religious reverence for life and love, in his striving for absolute freshness of perception and the utmost directness of statement, and in his stubborn refusal to subordinate the dictates of his poetic vision to the ever-shifting demands of totalitarian bureaucracy.

3.

In what is one of the most sensitive essays on Pasternak in English,[38] Helen Muchnic eloquently demonstrates the funda-

---

[37] *Ibid.*, p. 50.
[38] "Boris Pasternak and Yurii Zhivago," *From Gorky to Pasternak* (New York, 1961), pp. 341–404.

mental continuity of Pasternak's poetic vision from his earliest lyrics down to the *Doctor Zhivago* period. To be sure, the aging poet's much-touted repudiation of his early writings as " mere trifles " [39] need not be taken literally. Yet such *dicta* cannot be altogether ignored either, especially where Pasternak's image of himself as a poet is concerned. Nor can it be denied that in the late phase of his career a partial shift of moral emphasis, a discernible change in the scope of the Pasternakian universe did indeed occur.

In the language of the early Pasternak, this change could have been described as a sudden coalescence of two poles of reality—lyricism and history.[40] Viktor Frank, one of the most perceptive Russian *émigré* students of Pasternak, has put it a little differently: " A new dimension appeared in Pasternak's work, a social dimension." [41]

Once again, let us beware of simplifications. As I have already indicated, none of Pasternak's previous works is properly or meaningfully described by such terms as " asocial," or for that matter, " self-centered," to quote Il'ia Erenburg's characteristically ambivalent memoir.[42] The overflowing cosmic ecstasy of Pasternak's early verse, reaching as it does beyond the merely personal, militates against these labels. The fact remains, though, that in many a Pasternak lyric the poet, occasionally flanked by his beloved, is the only recognizable human protagonist. In the excited confrontation between the creator and his " sister, life " there is little room for others—for an explicit relatedness to, and active participation in, other human lives, for that sense of interconnectedness of human

---

[39] Pasternak's letter to a Uruguayan magazine editor, quoted by N. Chiaromonte in " Pasternak's Message," *Partisan Review* (Winter, 1958), pp. 127–34.

[40] In an early essay " A Black Cup " (1916) Pasternak says somewhat cryptically: " Reality disintegrates. In the process, it crystallizes around two opposite poles: Lyricism and History. Both are equally absolute and *a priori*." (*Sochineniia*, III, 150–51.)

[41] *Sbornik statei posviaschennykh B. L. Pasternaku* [A Miscellany devoted to B. L. Pasternak] (Munich, 1961), p. 349.

[42] *People and Life 1891–1921* (New York, 1962), pp. 278–86.

destinies,[43] which is part and parcel of the late Pasternak's—
and Iurii Zhivago's—Christian personalism.

> My desire is to be among people,
> And in crowds, in their bustle and ease
>
> .   .   .   .
>
> Just as though I were under their skin,
> I can feel all their thoughts as my own,
> And I melt as the melting of snow
> Like the morning my brows wear a frown.
>
> For with me are those without names,
> The homebody, the child, the tree,
> I am truly vanquished by them all . . .
> Therein lies my sole victory.[44]

This notion of self-transcendence as spiritual communion, as
being " vanquished " by or merging with others, a notion born
no doubt of the shared ordeal of " Russia's terrible years," is
bound up with another theme which is essentially new here.
The predicament of Iurii Zhivago clearly implies the inextricable connection between the fate of a man of sensibility
and imagination, in short, of a poet, and the moral texture of

---

[43] Pasternak, *Doctor Zhivago*, pp. 67–68.

[44] The above English rendition is a slightly modified version of Henry Kamen's
recent translation of " Daybreak," one of the poems of Iurii Zhivago (*In the
Interlude, Poems 1945–1960* [London, New York, 1962] p. 75).

> Мне к людям хочется, в толпу,
> В их утреннее оживленье.
>
> .   .   .   .
>
> Я чувствую за них за всех,
> Как будто побывал в их шкуре
> Я таю сам, как тает снег,
> Я сам, как утро, брови хмурю.
> Со мною люди без имен
> Деревья, дети, домоседы.
> Я ими всеми побежден,
> И только в том моя победа.

(Doktor Zhivago, pp. 557–58.)

his society. Though Pasternak's novel carefully avoids any narrowly political moral, the life and death of its main protagonist epitomizes the impossibility of poetry under the " reign of a lie," the inseparability of creative genius and freedom (Gerschenkron).[45] Once again the death of a poet becomes an indictment of a society, an ultimate proof of its spiritual enslavement. Once again the artist's right to creative integrity and emotional privacy appear as the embattled individual's last line of defense against the encroachments of the omnipotent state.

It is scarcely necessary to urge that the above represents not only the objective import of the novel, but the subjective intent of its author as well. Pasternak's increasing awareness of his role and responsibility as a spokesman for those who cannot speak was amply evidenced by his apparent determination to proclaim his message, to make his novel available to the world, whatever the cost to himself and those dearest to him.

" Mission," " testimony," " ordeal "—are we not back, after all, in Blok's and Maiakovskii's universe of discourse? Yes and no. The affinities between the author of *Doctor Zhivago* and Aleksandr Blok are all too apparent. Pasternak's affection for, and sense of indebtedness to the Symbolist spellbinder may have derived additional poignancy from the fact that he had lived through the fulfillment of Blok's apocalyptic prophecies. In the epilogue to *Doctor Zhivago* one of Iurii's surviving friends, Misha Gordon, muses thus: " When Blok was saying [in his much-quoted 1914 poem], ' We, children of Russia's terrible years,' the line was to be interpreted figuratively. The children were not children, terrors were not terrible, but providential, apocalyptic. Now the figurative has become literal, children are children, and terrors are terrible." [46] In *I Remember* Pasternak paid an eloquent tribute to Blok in words which

---

[45] " Creative freedom and genius are as inseparable as human life and human breath," A. Gerschenkron, *Economic Backwardness in Historical Perspective* (Cambridge, Mass., 1962).

[46] Boris Pasternak, *Doktor Zhivago* [in Russian] (Ann Arbor, 1957), p. 530.

could have been easily addressed to his own achievement: "Blok had everything that goes to make a great poet—fire, tenderness, emotion, his own image of the world, his own special gift for transforming everything he touched, and his own restrained, self-absorbed destiny." [47] In a lyrical triptych " The Wind," devoted to Blok's memory, he hailed the restless visionary as his generation's vital, indispensable companion. [48]

There remains, however, a residual yet significant difference of moral thrust and self-image. While Blok was a seer, Pasternak was—or became increasingly—a witness.

In his thoughtful commentary appended to the recent English translation of Pasternak's post-1945 verse, G. Katkov offers a relevant distinction: " The mission of the poet in Blok's day had been prophecy; in Pasternak's it becomes one of apostolic service." [49]

The analogy between Christ's Passion and the ordeal of Iurii Zhivago has been urged by a number of critics, on occasion, quite persuasively. Yet the point is easily overstated. Iurii Zhivago is all too human, all too fallible to be a Christ-figure. As Obolensky properly reminds us, " Pasternak's design lay not in making Zhivago Christ-like but in suggesting that his life and death acquire their true significance when they are illumined by the reality of Christ's sacrificial death and His Resurrection." [50]

Pasternak's hero falters, suffers, endures, struggles and goes

[47] *I Remember* (New York, 1959), pp. 49–50.

[48] If Pasternak's affinity for Blok seems to have increased over the years, his initial enthusiasm for Maiakovskii had been somewhat dampened. In *Safe Conduct* Maiakovskii appears as a culture hero, as an epitome of the poet, though even there Pasternak admits to being estranged and puzzled by his more flamboyant confrere's propagandistic bombast. In *I Remember* a sympathetic and remarkably apt description of Maiakovskii's early lyrics (" a poetry beautifully modelled, majestic, demonic, and, at the same time, infinitely doomed, perishing and almost calling for help ") is followed by a harsh rejection of the bulk of his post-1917 output. (See above, " The Dead Hand of the Future," p. 129.)

[49] Pasternak, *In the Interlude*, p. 241.

[50] " The Poems of Doctor Zhivago," *The Slavonic and East European Review*, XL, No. 94 (December, 1961), 135.

down in an unequal battle only to leave behind a batch of poems which, twenty years after his death, will sustain his countrymen in their overwhelming desire for freedom.[51] Thus, his sacrifice has not been in vain. His fate, not unlike his creator's served to document the ultimate triumph of the spirit over the brute force of circumstance. Yet however strategic the embattled poet's mission, however trying his ordeal, it is not his job to point the way to salvation. Is it perhaps because the task of saving mankind is left here to Jesus Christ?

Clearly, the difference I am trying to highlight involves matters other than the poet's view of his own calling. Though Maiakovskii's radicalism was Bohemian rather than Marxist, though Blok's Dionysian romance with the November revolution proved in the end a tragic misunderstanding, both poets shared the political revolutionary's basic eschatology, his hankering for a climactic event, a liberating cataclysm, a total transformation of reality. Pasternak's temperament had never been that of a Utopian. By 1950 he had less use than ever for the notion of a millennium. He had lived to see the utopian *élan* of the Russian radical intelligentsia debased into the doctrinaire madness of the 1930's. He had witnessed the hardening of the ideal of " reshaping life " into a tedious official cliché. Hence, perhaps the increasing distrust of ultimate goals and grand designs, shared by Zhivago and Lara, their profound conviction that life is more important than the meaning of life, hence the characteristic affinity of Iurii Andreevich for the unflamboyant, unprogrammatic stance of Pushkin and Chekhov. The late Pasternak's admiration for Tolstoy is amply documented.[52] Nor is there any question as to his indebtedness to Dostoevsky.[53] Yet there is good reason to assume that Zhivago

---

[51] See Pasternak, *Doktor Zhivago*, " The Epilogue," pp. 530–31.

[52] See especially the moving tribute to Tolstoy's faculty of passionate seeing in Pasternak's *I Remember*, p. 69.

[53] I am inclined to agree with Gleb Struve that on balance " *Doctor Zhivago* has more affinity with Dostoevski than with Tolstoy." (" Sense and Nonsense about Doctor Zhivago," *Studies in Russian and Polish Literature.* In honor of Wacłow Lednicki [The Hague, 1962], p. 234).

speaks for his creator when he opts for Pushkin's and Chekhov's
"shy unconcern" with "loud things," "the ultimate goals of
humanity and their own salvation." "Such immodesties were
not for them; their station was not high enough and they were
too busy." [Gogol, Dostoevsky and Tolstoy] "prepared themselves for death, sought meanings, drew up accounts, whereas
these others were to the end absorbed in the current particulari-
ties of the artist's calling and their life passed in recording its
passage, like another private particularity which was no one's
concern, and now this particularity turns out to be everybody's
business, like an apple that is plucked when it is ripe and
reaches usefulness of itself, and fills itself more and more with
sweetness and meaning." [54]

In this scheme of things the life of the artist is not a prefiguration of the *vita nuova*, a sacrificial leap from the wilder-
ness of an unbearable present into the promised land of an
infinitely beautiful future. It is rather a poignant exemplifica-
tion of basic human values, a telling restatement of eternal
verities, the holiness of life, the enduring beauty of love, the
indispensability of personal freedom, of "authenticity," of
fidelity to one's self. In the end Pasternak makes no special
claims for the poet as a human being. He doesn't expect him,
ostensibly, to lead a special kind of life. He simply urges him
to be himself, to be and remain fully, richly, and if need be,
defiantly human—in a word, "alive."

> And never for a single instant
> Betray your true self or pretend—
> But be alive and only living,
> And only living to the end.[55]

---

[54] Pasternak, *Doktor Zhivago*, p. 294, as quoted by Helen Muchnic, *From Gorky
to Pasternak*, pp. 393–94. (I am quoting the passage in Professor Muchnic's rendition since I consider it more accurate than the one found in the English translation
of the novel.)

[55] Quoted from Boris Pasternak, *In the Interlude*, p. 105.

И должен ни единой долькой
Не отступаться от лица,

It is a grim commentary on the nature of the regime in whose shadow Pasternak was fated to live for thirty years, and on the tenor of the age which his fellow poet Mandelshtam, termed a murderous beast,[56] that this ostensibly unspectacular program should have become a bone of contention and the source of an ordeal.

When all is said and done, in the late Pasternak's poetics as in his earlier statements, the last word belongs to poetry rather than the poet. If the claim made for the artist as man is modest—though in Soviet society this very modesty could have been a sign of quiet heroism—the poet's image-making power is exalted as a crucial, indeed central human faculty. The philosophy of history which informs *Doctor Zhivago* derives the meaning of each historical epoch not from the " sound and fury " of recorded political events, but from the era's major creative ferment. The " Poems of Iurii Zhivago " echo and reinforce the exuberant eulogy of the " wonder-working might " of the creative genius found in Pasternak's early lyrics. To Pasternak, the poetic image does not merely heighten or keep alive, as it renews, reshuffles and articulates, our perception of reality. It does not merely reveal the essence of each phenomenon. (" For things tear off their masks," says Pasternak in one of his early poems. " When they have a reason to sing," that is when they enter the realm of art.) [57] It helps make existence what it is. Without the transforming and articulating impact of poetry, the universe would have been a " dumb place." [58] As the world turns into words, as the matter becomes song, what would have otherwise remained inchoate, inert, and " deaf " acquires a form, a voice, a vibrancy. By the same

---

Но быть живым, живым и только,
Живым и только до конца.

(*Sochineniia*, III, 63.)

[56] See above, " The Double Image," p. 15.
[57] Pasternak, *Sochineniia*, I, 86.
[58] *Ibid*., " Opredelenie poezii " [A Definition of Poetry], p. 22.

token the poem does not merely verbalize our delight in existence; it makes nature itself aware of the joy which it is capable of generating:

> Surely it is my vocation,
> To prevent the loneliness
> Of distances, to keep the earth
> Outside the town from desolation.[59]

Poetry thus is more than mimesis, an imitation or recreation of the given; it is a co-creator of existence, " a catalyst of reality." [60] Is not this notion another echo of Romantic aesthetics? Undoubtedly. Yet here is a romanticism with a difference, a romanticism which sets more store by the artifact than by the *artifex*, which cares less for the myth of the poet than for the ineluctable reality of the poem.

---

[59] Pasternak, *In the Interlude*, " The Earth," p. 83.
> На то ведь и мое призванье
> Чтоб не скучали расстояньл,
> Чтобы за городскою гранью
> Земле не тосковать одной.

(Doktor Zhivago, p. 560.)

[60] Frank, " Vodianoi znak," *Sbornik statei posviashchennykh B. L. Pasternaku*, p. 248.

INDEX

A

Adamovich, Georgii, 107
Aeschylos: mentioned, 56
Akhmatova, Anna, 107
Alexandrine (period), 85, 86
Anacreon, 24
Anacreontic ode, 24
Anacreontic stance (in Pushkin), 23, 25, 29
Apollon (Russian Modernist journal), 71
Ariosto: mentioned, 56
Arnold, Matthew: quoted, 30; mentioned, 49 n
Artist: the myth of, 6; as demiurge, 7; as Faustian figure, 7; as magician 7, 8; double image of, 9; narcissism of, 51; bourgeois, 58; as rebel, 134; as seer, 134
Aseev, Nikolai: cited, 95

B

Babel, Isaak, 14
Bailey, Benjamin, 48
Bal'mont, Konstantin: as older symbolist, 70; compared to Briusov, 83; and the 1905 Revolution, 90
Baudelaire, Charles, 80, 137
Beat movement, 11
Belyi, Andrei: and the Revolution, 14, 90, 91, 93; as a memoir writer (on the Silver age), 69; on Briusov, 84; " Reminiscences about A. A. Blok," 85; and Futurism, 96; *St. Petersburg*, 110; and Blok, 116; mentioned, 71, 97, 109
Berlin, Sir Isaiah: cited, 17, on Pasternak, 137, 138

Bezymenskii, Aleksandr, 129
Blok, Aleksandr: and the Romantic conception of the poet, 11, 12; and the Revolution, 13, 14, 90, 93, 112; " On the Calling of the Poet," 36; on Pushkin, 36; 37; " On Lyric Poetry," 68; as a Dionysian, 71; and Briusov, 83, 85, 91; " Letters on Poetry," 100; " Verses about the Fair Lady," 100; " The Terrible World," 100, 105; " The Snow Mask," 100, 116, 119; and the " elements " (*stikhiia*), 101, 116; music, concept of in, 101–2, 119; and self-sacrifice, 101, 111, 118; " The Twelve," 101, 110, 112–17; " The Soul of a Writer," 102; " The Intelligentsia and the Revolution," 102, 113; eroticism in, 103; " The Stranger," 103; " The Native Land," 103, 107; " The City," 105, 110; " The Elements and Culture," 108; " The Intelligentsia and the People," 108; " Three Questions," 108; his sense of history, 109–10; criticized by Zinaida Gippius, 109, 115; " The Retribution " (quoted), 114; " The Scythians," 115; " On the Kulikovo Field," 115, 119; " Carmen," 116, 119; " To the Muse," 119; his intonational pattern, 119; " In the Restaurant," 119
Bolshevism, Bolshevik, 14, 90, 95, 102, 112, 114, 115, 130
Bouneau, Sophie, 103
Bowra, Sir Cecil Maurice, 103
Brecht, Bertold, 13; quoted, 120
Briusov, Valerii: as older Symbolist, 70; on the essence of Symbolism, 71; as a Parnassian, 71, 83; " To the Poet," 72–75, 77, 80, 88; his pride compared to Pushkin's, 73; " The Poet to the Muse," 76; *Stephanos*, 78; *Urbi et*

155

THE DOUBLE IMAGE
Concepts of the Poet
in Slavic Literatures

by Victor Erlich

designer: Athena Blackorby
typesetter: J. H. Furst Co.
typefaces: Scotch, Deepdene
printer: J. H. Furst Co.
paper: Warren's 1854
binder: Albrecht Co.
cover material: Bancroft Arrestox C